Stay on
POINT

Jack McBain

1

DARAKWON

Stay on
POINT ①

Author Jack McBain
Publisher Chung Kyudo
Editors Kwak Bitna, Cho Sangik
Designers Park Bohee, Lee Seunghyun

First Published October 2018
By Darakwon Inc.
Darakwon Bldg., 211, Munbal-ro, Paju-si, Gyeonggi-do 10881
Republic of Korea

Tel. 82-2-736-2031 (Ext. 553)

Price ₩13,000
ISBN 978-89-277-0962-6 14740
     978-89-277-0961-9 14740 (set)
http://www.darakwon.co.kr

Main Book / Free MP3 Available Online
7 6 5 4 3 2 1   18 19 20 21 22

Introduction

Stay on Point 1 is the first book in a two-level series for English language learners interested in learning basic techniques of oral presentations. Not only is this book appropriate for beginner-level students who are new to these concepts, but it also serves as a helpful guide for those wanting to review speechwriting basics. The information in this book is essential for any high school student, university student, or professional person who might at some point need to prepare and deliver a speech in English. The information found in this series will not only prove helpful to English language learners hoping to improve their oral presentation skills but will also offer a glimpse into Western culture and the norms and traditions associated with public speaking in the West.

Stay on Point 1 contains twelve units, which cover a variety of topics. Each unit consists of language-building exercises, a new presentation skill, and an outline for students to follow as they craft oral presentations of their own. Students will learn how to speak to inform as well as how to speak to persuade. Students will encounter topics such as *My Most Precious Object*, *Sports and Exercise*, and *Manmade Processes or Inventions*. By including topics in the book which are interesting and relevant to a student's life, we believe we can make the speechwriting process easier and more enjoyable.

Stay on Point 1 is a speech-preparation textbook which includes the steps necessary to write and deliver a speech from a Western academic perspective. The step-by-step approach in this book allows students to craft and deliver high-quality academic speeches on a wide variety of topics. Each unit introduces readers to a new aspect of the speech-preparation process. As students come to the end of a unit, they will find that they have added another tool to their speechwriting toolkit. Each unit in the book gradually becomes more challenging as students are asked to apply knowledge they learned in the previous units to the current one. The vocabulary, language-learning, pronunciation, and reading sections give students a chance to improve their overall linguistic skills. Communicative tasks, such as pair work and class activities, provide students with opportunities to apply what they have learned in the language-building sections to authentic speaking situations. Each unit aims to help students build confidence and gain competence as they develop their oral presentation skills.

Author's Acknowledgments

The author would like to express his most sincere gratitude to the editor Bitna Kwak. Without her tireless work and guidance, this project would not have been possible. He would also like to acknowledge the contributions of Mr. Michael Putlack and the entire Darakwon management and staff. Finally, he would like to extend a heartfelt thanks to his family, who has been incredibly patient during the writing process of this book.

Scope and Sequence

Unit	Learning Outcomes	Vocabulary
Unit 1 **People** p.8-15 Jobs Appearance and Personality Likes and Dislikes	Students can . . . talk about jobs describe appearances and personalities talk about likes and dislikes make a mind map prepare an informative speech about a friend or family member	Common jobs Adjectives for describing physical appearance and personalities
Unit 2 **Precious Objects** p.16-23 Descriptive Adjectives The Five Senses Family Heirlooms	Students can . . . describe an object describe how things look, feel, sound, smell, and taste talk about family heirlooms jot down notes prepare an informative speech about a precious object	Descriptive adjectives The five senses
Unit 3 **Houses or Apartments** p.24-31 Items in a House or an Apartment Expressing Spatial Relations My First Home	Students can . . . name the items in a house or an apartment say where objects are in relation to one another describe their first home practice free-writing prepare an informative speech about a house or an apartment	The rooms and items in a house or an apartment
Unit 4 **Holidays** p.32-39 Holiday Dates and Customs Expressing Feelings and the Causes of Feelings My Holiday Traditions	Students can . . . say the dates of holidays and describe holiday customs express their feelings and talk about the causes of feelings describe holiday traditions write an attention-getting opener prepare an informative speech about a favorite holiday	Famous holiday dates -ed and -ing adjectives
Unit 5 **Food and Drinks** p.40-47 Giving Clear Instructions Using Ordinal Numbers and Sequence Adverbs Why I Like Making It / Why I Like It	Students can . . . give instructions about how to make a food or drink describe the steps in a process talk about why they like making or consuming a favorite food or drink write more attention-getting openers prepare an informative speech about a favorite food or drink	Verbs related to cooking Ordinal numbers Sequence adverbs Reasons for liking and making a food or drink
Unit 6 **Sports and Exercise** p.48-55 Sports and Exercise Equipment What Are the Benefits? Where to Do an Activity and Why	Students can . . . name a common sport or exercise talk about a sport or exercise talk about sports and exercise equipment talk about where and why they do a sport or exercise create a PowerPoint presentation prepare a speech about a favorite sport or exercise	Names of sports and exercise Names of sports and exercise equipment Do, go, and play

Grammar	Language Patterns	Pronunciation	Reading	Learning How	Do It Yourself
Wh-question words	Describing a person's appearance and personality	/p/, /f/, /b/, and /v/ sounds	People's likes and dislikes	Brainstorming with mind maps	Describe a person
Adjectives	Using sense verbs	/s/ and /z/ sounds	Family heirlooms	Brainstorming by jotting down notes	Describe a precious object
There is / There are	Prepositions of place	Common reductions of *for*, *and*, and *or*	Descriptions of people's homes	Brainstorming by free-writing	Describe a house or an apartment
Adverbs of frequency	Using *-ed* and *-ing* adjectives	Common reductions of *him* and *her*	Holiday traditions	Writing the attention-getting opener	Describe a holiday
The imperative mood	Using ordinal numbers and sequence adverbs	Common reductions of *want to*, *going to*, and *got to*	Why I like making a food or drink Why I like a food or drink	Writing the attention-getting opener (continued)	Describe a food or drink
Using *must, must not, have to*, and *don't have to*	Collocations for *do*, *go*, and *play*	/θ/ and /ð/ sounds	Where and why to do a sport or exercise	Creating a good PowerPoint presentation	Describe a sport or exercise

Unit	Learning Outcomes	Vocabulary
Unit 7 **Natural Processes** p.56-63 Life Cycles The Stages of Growth in a Life Cycle The Positives and Negatives of a Natural Process	Students can . . . identify natural processes explain the stages in a natural process describe the positives and negatives of a natural process create well-made PowerPoint slides prepare a speech in which they describe a natural process	Living organisms Stages of growth and development in living organisms Life cycles
Unit 8 **Manmade Processes or Inventions** p.64-71 Inventors and Inventions Cause and Effect How It Works	Students can . . . name some famous inventors name some popular inventions and innovations explain a cause and its effect explain how an invention or a manmade process works use notecards in a speech prepare a speech in which they describe an invention or a manmade process	Names of inventors and inventions Cause and effect
Unit 9 **Opinions** p.72-79 Making Comparisons Giving Your Opinion Personal Experience	Students can . . . make comparisons give opinions and state preferences talk about their personal experiences learn how to choose a good persuasive speech topic prepare a speech about why one object or method is better than another	Opposite adjectives
Unit 10 **Beliefs** p.80-87 Myths and Misconceptions Stating Facts Supporting Facts	Students can . . . identify common myths and misconceptions state facts in a speech provide supporting facts and evidence in a speech write a persuasive claim prepare a speech in which they challenge a common belief	Common myths and misconceptions
Unit 11 **Behaviors** p.88-95 Problems and Solutions Giving Advice Supporting Details and Information	Students can . . . identify good and bad habits and behaviors identify problems and their solutions give advice find evidence to support their claim write a persuasive claim while building on an area of agreement prepare a speech encouraging someone to change a behavior	Good and bad habits Positive and negative behaviors Giving advice
Unit 12 **Research and Visual Aids** p.96-103 Conducting Research Citing Sources Discussing Visual Aids	Students can . . . identify different charts and graphs conduct research in preparation for the speech cite sources in a speech describe and discuss a visual aid describe changes in a chart or graph prepare a speech in which they use a visual aid such as a chart or graph	Charts and graphs Resources for doing research Citing sources Changes in charts and graphs

Grammar	Language Patterns	Pronunciation	Reading	Learning How	Do It Yourself
The present perfect tense	The stages in a natural process	/l/ and /r/ sounds	The positives and negatives of a natural process	Creating a good PowerPoint presentation (continued)	Describe a natural process
The active voice and the passive voice	Cause and effect	/d/, /t/, and /ld/ sounds	How a manmade process works	Using notecards	Describe a manmade proces, or an invention
Comparative adjectives	Expressing opinions	/s/, /z/, and /lz/ sounds	Describing preferences	Choosing a good persuasive speech topic	Give a speech about why one object or method is better than another
Using the verb "do"	Stating facts	Common reductions of "It's a..." "He's a..." and "She's a..."	Interesting facts that might not be well known	Writing a good persuasive claim	Give a speech in which you challenge a common belief
Using the bare infinitive when giving advice	Giving advice	Common reductions of *shouldn't have* and *shouldn't*	A positive behavior and a negative behavior	Building on areas of agreement	Give a speech encouraging someone to change a behavior
Reported speech	Citing sources in a speech	Common pronunciations of 13, 14, 15, 16, 17, 18, 19 and 30, 40, 50, 60, 70, 80, 90	Discussing information in a chart or graph	Describing changes in charts and graphs	Give an informative or persuasive speech which includes a visual aid

People

Warm-up

Read the various introductions. Then introduce yourself to the group.

Hi! I'm Kara, and I'm 39 years old. I'm from Australia. Actually, I was born in England, but my parents moved to Australia when I was thirteen. How are you going?

Hello! I'm Young. I'm 21 years old, and I'm from South Korea. I feel really nervous when I speak in public. Um... that's all, I guess.

Hey, everyone! I'm Tyrell, and I'm 32 years old. I'm from the United States. I love speaking in public. That's why I'm a professional motivational speaker.

YOU

Jobs When introducing someone to a group, we can begin by telling the group about what the person does for a living. We can give the group the person's job title and then add a description of the person's workplace and job responsibilities.

Vocabulary

A Match the jobs with the correct definitions.

1 office worker •   • a a person who helps people invest their money wisely

2 store manager •   • b a person who makes sure the daily operations of a business run smoothly

3 app developer •   • c a person who creates and publishes original content for one or more media platforms

4 sales clerk •   • d a person who files documents, writes reports, and does other office tasks

5 banker •   • e a person who writes programs for computers

6 content creator •   • f a person who creates software applications

7 computer programmer •   • g a person who sells merchandise in a retail store

B **Pair work** | Talk about the job responsibilities related to the jobs in A with your partner by using the definitions.

A What are office workers' job responsibilities?

B They have to file documents, write reports, and do other office tasks.

Grammar

A Let's learn about *wh*-question words.

What / Who / Where / When / Why

A **What** do you do for fun?

B I play basketball.

A **Who** do you play basketball with?

B I play basketball with my friends.

A **Where** do you play?

B We play at the park.

A **When** do you play?

B We play every weekend.

A **Why** don't you play during the week?

B Because we are really busy during the week.

B Complete the questions with the correct *wh*-question words.

A ___What___ do you do?

B I'm a professor.

A ¹_____ are your job responsibilities?

B I prepare lessons, mark exams, and teach.

A ²_____ do you work?

B I work at a university.

A ³_____ do you work there?

B I enjoy working there, so that's why I do it.

A ⁴_____ do you work?

B I only teach on Mondays, Wednesdays, and Fridays.

A ⁵_____ do you work with?

B I work with two other colleagues.

Appearance and Personality When describing someone to a group, we can include descriptions of the person's physical appearance as well as that person's personality traits. This gives the listener a more accurate idea of the person being described.

Language Patterns

A Let's learn some language patterns.

He/She is + adjective	He/She has + adjective + noun
He is muscular.	She has red hair.
He is boring.	She has fair skin.
She is intelligent.	He has blue eyes.

B **Pair work** | Write the names of three people you know and choose words from the boxes to make true sentences about them. Then share your sentences with your partner.

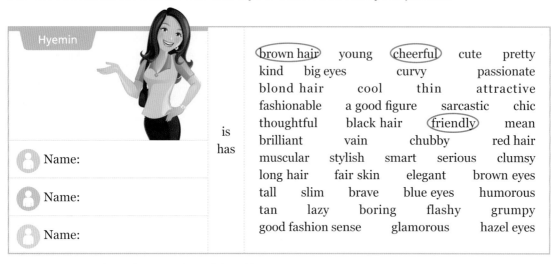

Hyemin

Name:

Name:

Name:

is
has

brown hair   young   cheerful   cute   pretty
kind   big eyes   curvy   passionate
blond hair   cool   thin   attractive
fashionable   a good figure   sarcastic   chic
thoughtful   black hair   friendly   mean
brilliant   vain   chubby   red hair
muscular   stylish   smart   serious   clumsy
long hair   fair skin   elegant   brown eyes
tall   slim   brave   blue eyes   humorous
tan   lazy   boring   flashy   grumpy
good fashion sense   glamorous   hazel eyes

Hyemin has brown hair. She is friendly and cheerful.

Pronunciation ◉

A Read and listen to the words below. Then practice the pronunciations of the /p/, /f/, /b/, and /v/ sounds.

/p/	/f/	/b/	/v/
passionate	**f**ashionable	**b**oastful	**v**engeful
de**p**endable	de**f**ensive	**b**road	**v**aliant
pretty	**f**inicky	**b**rilliant	**v**ain
proud	**f**unky	**b**lue	**v**iolent

B Listen and practice. Be careful when pronouncing the /p/, /f/, /b/, and /v/ sounds.

1 She has wa**v**y **b**lond hair. And she is **p**retty.

2 The **p**retty woman in the **p**ink **b**louse isn't **v**ain.

3 The **b**lond **b**oy in the **b**lue shorts is a little **f**at.

Likes and Dislikes When introducing someone, we can talk about the person's likes and dislikes. By discussing the person's favorite and least favorite activities, we can get to know the person on a deeper level. We should include when, where, why, and with whom they enjoy doing their favorite activities.

Reading 🔊

A **Read about the following people's likes and dislikes.**

I am Kevin, and I like playing games. Actually, I don't like sports at all. I like games that challenge my mind. On weekends, I usually go to Central Park and play chess. Chess teaches you about strategy, and I find that very interesting. I really dislike watching television. I think it is a waste of time. I don't like listening to music either. I'd much rather listen to a lecture from a really intelligent professor.

I'm Andrea, and I really love to go shopping. My friends say I'm a shopaholic. I go shopping two or three times a week. On weekends, I might visit nine or ten stores in one day. None of my friends can keep up with me. I really hate working at my part-time job. I'm a sales clerk in a convenience store. It's really boring, but I need the job so I can go shopping on the weekends!

Following the Reading Write about your own likes and dislikes.

• My Likes:

• My Dislikes:

B **Pair work** | Write some of your likes and dislikes in the circles. Then ask your partner what he or she thinks about your items.

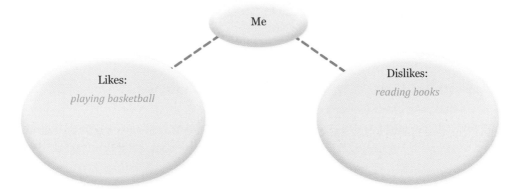

A I like playing basketball. What do you think about it?

B I love it, too. I play basketball every Saturday morning.

A I don't like reading books. How about you?

B I don't like reading, either. I'd rather watch movies.

Learning How

Brainstorming with Mind-maps When writing a speech, it is important to begin by brainstorming. Brainstorming helps you unlock the many different ideas you have surrounding a single topic. Once the ideas begin to flow, a mind map helps you manage your creative output in an organized way.

A Look at the two different versions of mind maps. Then complete notes for each person.

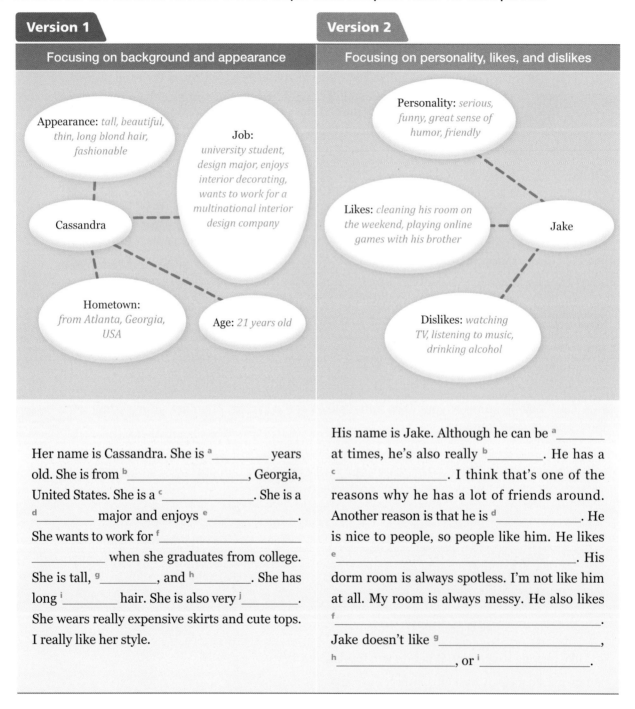

Version 1

Focusing on background and appearance

Appearance: *tall, beautiful, thin, long blond hair, fashionable*

Job: *university student, design major, enjoys interior decorating, wants to work for a multinational interior design company*

Cassandra

Hometown: *from Atlanta, Georgia, USA*

Age: *21 years old*

Version 2

Focusing on personality, likes, and dislikes

Personality: *serious, funny, great sense of humor, friendly*

Likes: *cleaning his room on the weekend, playing online games with his brother*

Jake

Dislikes: *watching TV, listening to music, drinking alcohol*

Her name is Cassandra. She is ª_____ years old. She is from ᵇ_____, Georgia, United States. She is a ᶜ_____. She is a ᵈ_____ major and enjoys ᵉ_____. She wants to work for ᶠ_____ _____ when she graduates from college. She is tall, ᵍ_____, and ʰ_____. She has long ⁱ_____ hair. She is also very ʲ_____. She wears really expensive skirts and cute tops. I really like her style.

His name is Jake. Although he can be ª_____ at times, he's also really ᵇ_____. He has a ᶜ_____. I think that's one of the reasons why he has a lot of friends around. Another reason is that he is ᵈ_____. He is nice to people, so people like him. He likes ᵉ_____. His dorm room is always spotless. I'm not like him at all. My room is always messy. He also likes ᶠ_____. Jake doesn't like ᵍ_____, ʰ_____, or ⁱ_____.

B Use the picture and the speech to help you complete the mind maps with information about Amanda's appearance, and Scott's personality, likes, and dislikes. You don't need to use complete sentences in the bubbles.

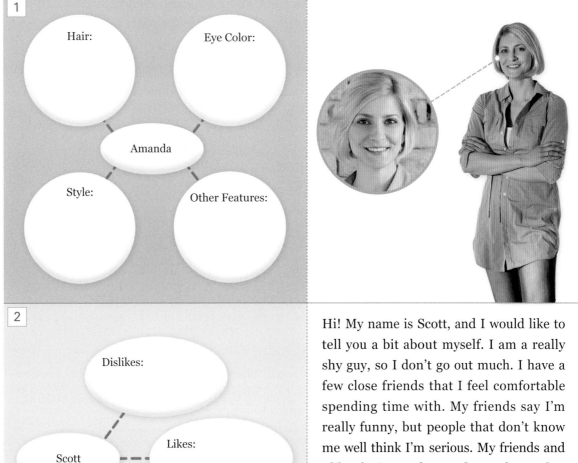

1

Hair:

Eye Color:

Amanda

Style:

Other Features:

2

Dislikes:

Scott

Likes:

Personality:

Hi! My name is Scott, and I would like to tell you a bit about myself. I am a really shy guy, so I don't go out much. I have a few close friends that I feel comfortable spending time with. My friends say I'm really funny, but people that don't know me well think I'm serious. My friends and I like playing cards. We play cards together every Friday night. I also like riding my bike. I ride my bike for two hours every day. I don't like playing team sports. I also don't like watching sports on television. I love watching movies. My favorite movie genre is science fiction.

💡 **Common Mistakes be vs. have**

Sujin is beautiful. She is a teacher. (The "be" verb is a connecting verb.)

Sujin has brown hair, and she has brown eyes. (= Her hair and eyes are brown.)

Do It Yourself

The Descriptive Speech: People Now it is time for you to do it yourself! Use the information you learned in the previous sections in order to create an outline for a speech describing a person.

A Choose one of the mind maps below to complete notes about your person.

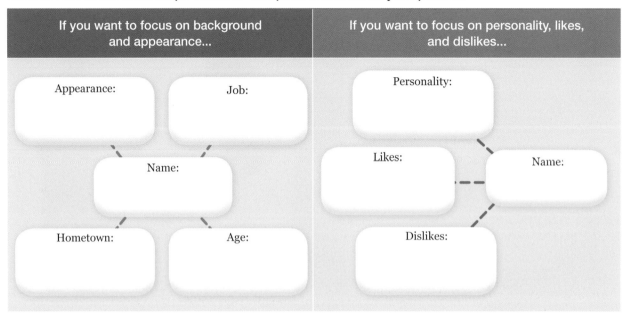

If you want to focus on background and appearance...	If you want to focus on personality, likes, and dislikes...
Appearance: Job: Name: Hometown: Age:	Personality: Likes: Name: Dislikes:

B Make notes by using the information from the mind map.

C Give a short speech about a person. Use one of the introduction and conclusion examples in the bubbles.

Introduction
(a) Let me tell you about our classmate.
(b) I would like to introduce my friend.
(c) I'd like to tell you about my sister.

Body (Speech Notes)

Conclusion
(a) I have told you a little about our classmate.
(b) Thank you for listening.
(c) I've introduced you to my sister. Thank you for your time.

Checklist

1 What are the five *wh*-question words mentioned in the unit?
2 What can you discuss if you want to give a good description of a person?
3 What is the benefit of discussing a person's likes and dislikes in a descriptive speech?
4 Do you need to write in complete sentences when making a mind map?
5 What part of the speech will the mind map categories help the speechwriter create?
6 What are the three main parts of a speech?

Presentation Tips

Making Eye Contact

Reading your speech is not the best strategy to use when giving a speech. Speeches that are read word for word can come across as robotic or stiff to an audience. You want your speech to be conversational, and that's not possible when reading a speech to an audience. You also want to make eye contact with your audience. The audience will be much more receptive to your speech if they feel like you are talking to them. Good public speakers make the audience feel like the speaker is making a personal connection with them. This connection is only possible through the use of eye contact and a conversational speaking style. Glancing at your notes is okay, but reading a speech without making eye contact will most likely result in the audience losing interest in your speech. Besides, if you are just planning to read your speech to the audience, why not just give them a copy to read for themselves?

Precious Objects

Warm-up

Read about each person's most precious object and then fill in the blanks with the words from the word box.

| gift | grandmother | guitar | hat | necklace | army | ring | wedding |

My most precious object is my engagement _____. Every time I look at it, I think about how beautiful my _____ will be.

My parents bought this _____ for me for Christmas ten years ago. It's important to me because it was a _____ from my parents.

My mother gave me this _____ when I was 16 years old. Her mother, my _____, gave it to her when she turned 16.

My brother joined the _____ when he was 19 years old. The night before he left, he gave me his favorite _____. I wear it all the time because it reminds me of him.

Descriptive Adjectives When describing an object to a group, we should choose good descriptive adjectives. Try not to use the same words over and over again. Instead, use synonyms, words that have the same or similar meanings.

Vocabulary

A Write the words in the word box next to their synonyms in the sentences.

antique	broken	gigantic	inexpensive	miniature	valuable

1 My watch looks expensive, but it was actually quite **cheap** (_____). It was only $9.99.

2 Myrna's smartphone was **damaged** (_____) because she dropped it on the floor.

3 My mother gave me this necklace. It's made of gold, and it's very **expensive** (_____).

4 Kang's grandmother has a **huge** (_____) mirror in her living room.

5 Chen's uncle collects and restores **old** (_____) cars.

6 Saydee bought some **tiny** (_____) furniture for her dollhouse.

B **Pair work** | Talk to your partner about objects related to the words in A.

A Can you think of something cheap?

B Yes, I can. A pack of gum is cheap.

Grammar

A Let's learn about adjectives.

Most adjectives come before nouns.	Adjectives come after connecting verbs such as *be*, *look*, *feel*, and *seem*.
My uncle restores **old** cars. My dad gave me this **valuable** guitar. My grandmother has an **antique** clock.	This watch looks **cheap**. This silk feels **expensive**. Her mother's necklace is **beautiful**.

B Check the number where the adjective should be placed in each sentence.

1 strange   Hugh (1) bought a (2) painting.

2 colorful   Alexis's (1) dress is bright and (2).

3 bored   Your dog looks (1), so let's (2) take it for a walk.

4 exquisite   My father's (1) most precious object is the (2) piece of china in the living room.

5 fast   Bob's (1) new computer is (2).

C **Pair work** | Say these adjectives out loud to your partner. Then write down the name of the first object that comes to your partner's mind.

antique	valuable	tiny	beautiful

The Five Senses We can use verbs related to the five senses to describe things. We can ask ourselves what an object feels like, smells like, sounds like, looks like, and in the case of a food item, what it tastes like. The answers to these questions give us more information about an object.

Language Patterns

A Let's learn about connecting verbs related to the five human senses.

Touch	This cloth **feels** soft. This wood **feels** authentic.
Smell	My grandmother's apple pie **smells** great. The gloves **smell** like real leather.
Hearing	This piano **sounds** out of tune. The band's new album **sounds** great.
Sight	This painting doesn't **look** expensive. You **look** tired.
Taste	My aunt's homemade cookies **taste** amazing. This candy bar **tastes** too sweet.

B Write the names of five objects and make true sentences about them by using the sense verbs.

objects	sense verbs	adjectives
	feels	
	smells	
	sounds	
	looks	
	tastes	

Pronunciation 🔊

A Read and listen to the words below. Then practice the pronunciations of the /s/ and /z/ sounds.

/s/ (unvoiced)		/z/ (voiced)	
object**s**	think**s**	adjective**s**	sound**s**
look**s**	collect**s**	feel**s**	item**s**
taste**s**	make**s**	smell**s**	give**s**

B Listen and practice. Be careful when pronouncing the /s/ and /z/ sounds.

1 **S**ally'**s s**paghetti **s**mell**s s**o good.

2 **S**am look**s s**ad today. What'**s** the matter with him?

3 **S**umin'**s** cookie ta**s**te**s** better than **S**arah'**s** brownie.

4 Her daughter feel**s s**ick today, **s**o **s**he i**s**n't going to go to **s**chool.

5 **S**hin'**s** necklace look**s** more expen**s**ive than Rhett'**s** bracelet.

Building Content ❸

Family Heirlooms A family heirloom is a precious item that is passed from one generation to the next. Family heirlooms get their value from the meaningfulness of the objects. A silver ring that was given to you by a parent might be more meaningful than a gold one that you bought at a jewelry store.

Reading 🔊

A   Read about the following people's family heirlooms.

This jade necklace has been in my family for several generations. My great-great grandmother gave it to my great-grandmother when she turned 13 years old. My great-grandmother gave it to my grandmother when she turned 13, and my grandmother gave it to my mother when my mother turned 13. Tomorrow is my 13ᵗʰ birthday, and I think my mother is going to give it to me. I'm so excited!

- Sumin

I found this antique doll in our attic this morning. I asked my mother about it, and she said it was her mother's doll. My mom told me that my great-grandfather gave it to my grandmother when she was a child. My grandmother got really sick, so to make my grandmother feel better, her father gave her this doll. I think the story is very sweet, but the doll looks extremely scary.

- April

My mom and dad bought me this guitar when I was a freshman in college. I was really lonely because I lived so far away from home. My parents thought I needed a hobby, so they gave me a guitar. Now I love playing the guitar, and when my son turns 18 years old, I'm going to give it to him.

- Jonathon

Following the Reading   Answer the questions.

1   Who was the first person to receive Sumin's family heirloom?

2   When will Sumin probably receive the heirloom from her mother?

3   What does April think about her family heirloom?

4   What is Jonathon going to do when his son turns 18?

B   **Pair work |** Ask about a family heirloom. Then tell your partner about your family heirloom.

A What is your family heirloom?

B It's a snow globe. My grandmother gave it to me.

A Why is it special?

B She got it from her father, my great-grandfather, 50 years ago...

Brainstorming: Jotting Down Notes Another effective brainstorming strategy is jotting down notes. Start with a blank notepad or a piece of paper. Decide what the main points of the speech are. Then jot down ideas that relate to the main points. It is okay to jot down sentence fragments and words.

A Look at John's notes about his grandfather's pocket watch. Then complete the script by using the information in the notes.

Why It's Precious

- heirloom from my great-grandfather
- bought it at a watch shop in London during WWII
- cost 100 pounds
- passed down from one generation to the next
- got it from my dad when I was 16

Description of the Pocket Watch

- small, round, a little heavy, gold, expensive, old, antique
- glass face is scratched, watch doesn't work anymore
- watch stopped working 30 years ago

Speech Notes (Body of the Speech)

To begin with, I'd like to talk about why this watch is precious to me. It was my [1]_____ watch. He bought it at a watch shop in [2]_____ during [3]_____. It cost [4]_____ pounds. This watch has been passed down from one generation to the next in my family. My dad gave it to me when I was [5]_____. Now, I'd like to describe the pocket watch to you in more detail. It is [6]_____ and round, and it feels a little [7]_____ because it is made of gold. Because it is made of gold, it looks quite [8]_____, too! The pocket watch is old, so you could say it is an [9]_____ watch. The glass face is [10]_____, and it doesn't work anymore. My dad told me that it stopped telling time about [11]_____ ago. My father decided not to fix it. Now that I own the watch, I'm thinking about taking it to a watch shop. But everyone uses their phones to tell the time these days, so I might not get it fixed.

B   Use the reading and the picture to help you complete the notes about Abby's most precious object. Use the reading to make notes about why the necklace is important to her, and use the photo to make descriptive notes about the necklace. Only write down the most important information.

1

My mother has a lot of beautiful necklaces, but her heart necklace is my favorite. I don't like it because it's the most beautiful. It isn't. Her pearl necklace is much more beautiful. But it does have the most interesting backstory. My mother bought the necklace in Germany in 1999. She studied abroad when she was a junior in college. It's also a locket, so the heart opens up to show a picture of my mom when she was an exchange student in Germany. She was so beautiful. The last reason I love it is that my mom used to wear it a lot when I was young. My mom told me that I used to try to take it from her neck when I was a baby.

Why the Necklace Is
Important to Me

• *from Germany*

•

•

2

Necklace Description

• *chic*

•

•

•

•

🐞 **Common Mistakes Ordering Adjectives (quantity, value, size, age, shape, color, material)**

two large gold rings	(correct)	two gold large rings	(incorrect)
a small, round white pearl	(correct)	a white round small pearl	(incorrect)
three ugly, old pocket watches	(correct)	ugly three old pocket watches	(incorrect)

Do It Yourself

The Descriptive Speech: Precious Objects Now it is time for you to do it yourself! Use the information you learned in the previous sections in order to create an outline for a speech describing a precious object.

A Use the notepads below to jot down notes about your most precious object.

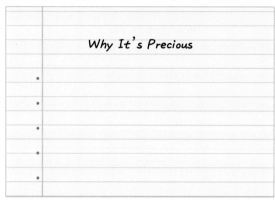

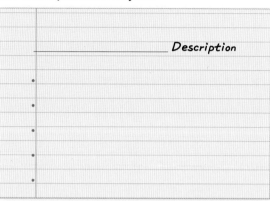

B Write a short speech script by using your notes from A.

Speech Notes (Body of the Speech)

To begin with, I'd like to talk about...

Now, I'd like to describe...

C Give a short speech about a precious object.

Introduction
I'd like to talk about my most precious object. It's my...

Body
To begin with, I'd like to talk about...
Now, I'd like to describe...

Conclusion
That concludes my speech about my most precious object.
Thank you for listening.

Checklist

1 What kinds of words can be helpful when describing an object to an audience?
2 What should we try to avoid when using descriptive language?
3 What are the five verbs for human senses mentioned in the unit?
4 What brainstorming strategy is discussed in the unit?
5 Is it okay to jot down only words or sentence fragments when brainstorming?

Presentation Tips

Previewing the Main Points of a Speech

Informative and persuasive speeches must include a preview of the main points. The preview should come at the end of the introduction. We preview the main points of a speech because we want to give the audience a roadmap for the speech. Audiences can be very picky, especially when it comes to listening to a speech. By previewing the main points, you are giving the audience an outline of the body of your speech. A preview lets the audience know what to expect, how many main points you are planning to discuss, and what the subtopic for each main point is. You want to avoid cramming all of the information in the body of your speech together without any separation. The body of the speech must be broken up into digestible pieces for the audience. Once you have determined what the main points in the body of the speech are going to be, you should briefly preview each one in the introduction. You can preview the main points by saying something like this: "First, I'd like to discuss (A). Next, I will talk about (B). Last, I will talk about (C). Now, let's talk about (A)."

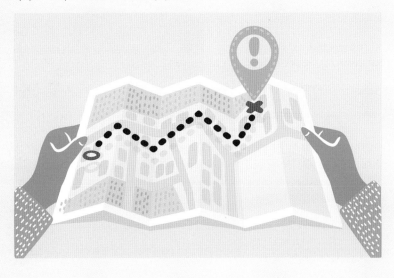

Houses or Apartments

Warm-up

A Label the rooms with their correct names.

| bathroom | bedroom | dining room | garage | kitchen | living room |

1

2

3

4

5

6

B   Do you live in an apartment or a house? Which of the rooms above do you have in your home?

Items in a House or an Apartment When describing your house or apartment, you should include a list of some of the important items in your home. This will give the listener a mental picture of the interior of your house or apartment.

Vocabulary

A Match the items commonly found in a home with their correct pictures on the map.

a. refrigerator	b. sofa	c. dining table	d. chair	e. stove	f. bathtub
g. bed	h. toilet	i. sink (x 2)	j. microwave	k. television	l. desk
m. bookcase	n. coffee table	o. car		p. wardrobe/closet	

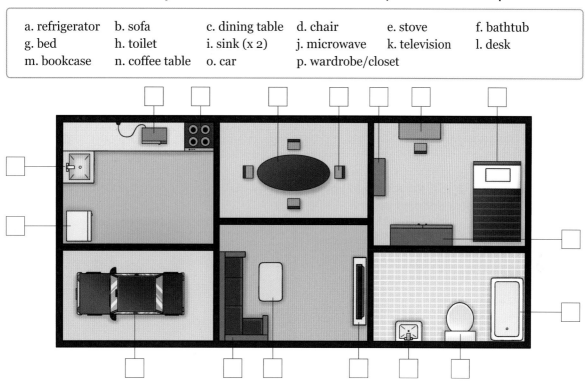

B **Pair work** | Ask your partner what items there are in his or her bedroom.

A What's in your bedroom?

B There's a bed in my bedroom. There are also a wardrobe, a desk, a chair, and a bookcase. There isn't a television.

Grammar

A Let's learn about *There is* and *There are*.

There is + singular nouns and uncountable nouns	There are + plural nouns
There is a coffee table in the living room. **Is there** a bathtub in the bathroom? **There isn't** any furniture in the new house yet.	**There are** some chairs in the dining room. **There aren't** any pillows on the bed. **Are there** any books in the bookcase?

B Complete the sentences with *There is*, *Is there*, *There are*, or *Are there*.

1 _____ some blankets on the sofa.

2 _____ a sink in the bathroom.

3 _____ any artwork in the living room?

4 _____ some pictures on the wall.

5 _____ not a bicycle in the garage.

6 _____ any shirts in the closet?

Expressing Spatial Relations When describing your house or apartment to a group of people, it is a good idea to use prepositions such as *in*, *on*, *across from*, *between*, *in front of*, and *next to* in order to express spatial relationships between certain objects in the house.

Language Patterns

A Let's practice using prepositions of place.

in, on, across from, between, in front of, next to

The sofa is **in** the living room.
The pillow is **on** the bed.
The bed is **across from** the bookcase.
The microwave is **between** the sink and the stove.
The coffee table is **in front of** the sofa.
The bathtub is **next to** the toilet.

B **Pair work** | Describe one of the rooms to your partner by using the prepositions in A. You and your partner should choose a different picture.

Pronunciation

A Read and listen to the sentences below. Then practice the common reductions of *for*, *and*, and *or*.

when written	when spoken
I bought a table **for** the living room.	I bought a table *fer* the living room.
The turkey **and** the pie are on the table.	The turkey *n* the pie are on the table.
Do you want wine **or** beer?	Do you want wine *er* beer?

B Listen and practice. Be careful when pronouncing *for*, *and*, and *or*.

1 Jane bought a sofa **for** the living room.

2 The TV **and** the coffee table are in the living room.

3 Jane will put the table in the dining room **or** the kitchen.

My First Home When describing your house or apartment to a group, you can give the audience some interesting facts about your home. This could include facts about the location of your home, some design features inside or outside your home, and even the personal significance your home has to you as the owner or renter.

Reading 🔊

A **Read about the following people's homes.**

This is my childhood home. It's located in the suburbs of Milwaukee, Wisconsin. It was small, but I loved this house because I grew up there. Isn't it cute? There were only two bedrooms, a living room, a kitchen, and one bathroom in the house. There was also a nice garden in the backyard. We lived in this house until I was 14 years old. Then, my family moved to a bigger house in the same city. I'm glad we live in a bigger house now, but I definitely miss our cute little house on Sandra Lane.

- Barbara / 21 years old

I grew up in an apartment in the city. My family lived on the top floor. The inside of the apartment was roomy and had unusually high ceilings. There were three bedrooms, a large kitchen, a large living room, and two bathrooms in the apartment. My mother and father bought the apartment before I was born. My family sold the apartment and moved to the country. But I will always miss the home I grew up in. Some of my friends still live in the neighborhood.

- Simon / 19 years old

Following the Reading Check the boxes that are correct.

Barbara's House	☐ small ☐ large ☐ 2 bedrooms ☐ 3 bedrooms ☐ 1 living room ☐ 1 bathroom ☐ suburbs ☐ city ☐ garden
Simon's Apartment	☐ small ☐ roomy ☐ 2 bedrooms ☐ 3 bedrooms ☐ 1 bathroom ☐ 2 bathrooms ☐ 1 small kitchen ☐ low ceilings ☐ high ceilings ☐ country ☐ downtown ☐ garden

B **Pair work** | What are three interesting facts about your childhood home? Introduce your childhood home to your partner by using these facts.

Brainstorming: Free-writing Another effective brainstorming strategy is free-writing. Start with a blank notepad or a piece of paper. Then, write down every idea that comes to mind. Don't edit out any of your ideas and try to keep your pen or pencil moving at the same speed as your thoughts.

A Read Karen's notes describing her apartment. Put a line through the unimportant information.

The Rooms and Their Spatial Relationships

There are five rooms in my house. There are a living room, a kitchen, a bedroom, a bathroom, and a dining room. The kitchen is next to the dining room. My kitchen is really dirty right now. I need to do the dishes. The dining room is next to the bedroom. The bedroom is across from the bathroom. The living room is across from the dining room. I wish my dining room were bigger.

The Items and Their Spatial Relationships

There are a bed, a closet, a desk, a chair, and a bookcase in the bedroom. The desk is next to the bookcase. I should reorganize my bookcase. The bookcase is across from the bed. The closet is next to the bed. There are a sofa, a coffee table, and a TV in the living room. The TV is across from the sofa. The coffee table is between the sofa and the TV. I think the television remote control is under the sofa. There are a fridge, a microwave, and a stove in the kitchen. I don't like cooking. There are a dining table and four chairs in the dining room.

Interesting Facts about My House

I bought this house two years ago. It's the first house I've ever owned. There is a cute garden in the backyard. My mother had a garden when I was young. I grow squash, kale, and strawberries in my garden. My house is near a school. The school has a soccer field and a basketball court. My house is only five years old, so it's pretty new. My house is painted red, but I'm thinking about painting it blue this summer. Blue is my favorite color.

B   Look at the picture of the apartment. Write about what rooms there are in the apartment and where they are in relation to one another. Then write about what items there are in the apartment and where they are located.

There are a bedroom, a living room, a kitchen...

C   Read about the items in the apartment. Then draw the items as they are described in the reading.

My Apartment

There are four rooms in my apartment. There are a living room, a kitchen, a bedroom, and a bathroom. There is a small sofa across from the television. There is a coffee table in front of the sofa. There is a refrigerator next to the sink in the kitchen. There is a table in front of the stove in the kitchen. There is a bed across from the wardrobe in the bedroom. And there is a toilet between the sink and the bathtub in the bathroom.

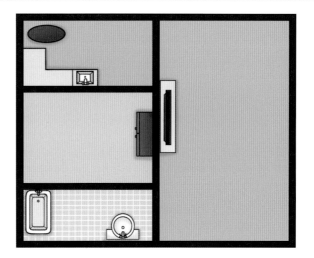

 Common Mistakes *There is* vs. *There are*

There **is** a sofa and a coffee table in the living room. (incorrect)

There **are** a sofa and a coffee table in the living room. (correct)

Do It Yourself

The Descriptive Speech: Houses or Apartments Now it is time for you to do it yourself! Use the information you learned in the previous sections in order to create an outline for a speech describing a house or an apartment.

A Use the notepads below to do a free-writing session in order to create the body of your speech. When you finish writing, delete the information from your notes that is not relevant to your speech.

B Give a short speech describing your house or apartment. Use your notes from A.

Introduction
Opening Remarks + Preview of Main Points
I'd like to describe my house/apartment for you today.
First, I will give you a layout of the rooms. Next, I will tell you where the furniture and other items are located. Last, I will tell you some interesting facts about the house/apartment.

Body
First, let's talk about the layout of the rooms...

Conclusion
That concludes my speech about my house/apartment.
Thank you for listening.

Checklist

1 Why should we include a list of the important items in a house or apartment?

2 According to the unit, what do prepositions do?

3 According to the unit, what kinds of interesting facts should we include when describing a house or an apartment?

4 What should we NOT do when free-writing?

Summarizing the Main Points of the Speech

Informative and persuasive speeches should include a summary of the main points. The summary should come at the beginning of the conclusion. We summarize the main points of a speech because we want to give the audience one last reminder of the main points covered in the body of the speech. In Western public speaking, there is an old joke that goes like this: "Tell the audience what you are going to tell them (a preview of the main points), tell them (the body), and tell them what you have told them (a summary of the main points)." For those who are new to public speaking, this idea can seem patronizing or disrespectful to the audience. In reality, we often need to hear things two or three times in order for the ideas to take root in our minds. In Western-style academic speaking, the number three appears several times as an organizational tool. There are three main parts to a speech: the introduction, the body, and the conclusion. We often include three main points in the body of a speech. With this in mind, a Western audience expects a speaker to provide them with a preview of the main points, the main points, and a summary of the main points.

Holidays

Warm-up

A Check the holidays you are familiar with.

B What's your favorite holiday and why?

Holiday Dates and Customs When describing a holiday or a special occasion, it is sometimes necessary to say the date of the holiday or the occasion. Some holidays fall on the same date every year, and others vary. We can also discuss the customs and traditions associated with a particular holiday.

Vocabulary

A Write the holidays next to the correct dates. Research the answers online if necessary.

> American Thanksgiving   Buddha's Birthday   Thai Songkran Festival
>
> Dia de los Muertos (Day of the Dead)   Ramadan   Christmas

1 November 28, 2019:

2 May 5, 2019 – June 4, 2019:

3 May 12th, 2019:

4 12/25:

5 4/13 – 4/15, 2019:

6 November 1st & 2nd:

B **Pair work** | Ask your partner when his or her birthday is. Then ask your partner what he or she usually does on his or her birthday.

A When's your birthday?

B It's January 25th.

A What do you usually do on your birthday?

B I usually go out to eat with my family. They usually bring a chocolate cake to the restaurant...

Grammar

A Let's learn about adverbs of frequency by reading the sentences about holiday customs.

100%	always	Easter is **always** celebrated on a Sunday.
	usually	The Chinese Lantern Festival **usually** falls in February or early March.
	often	South Koreans **often** eat rice cake soup on Lunar New Year's Day.
	sometimes	Americans **sometimes** go to a relative's home on Thanksgiving.
	not often	Children across the world **don't often** miss school on their birthdays.
0%	never	People **never** celebrate Christmas on December 26th.

*Adverbs come before main verbs and after the "be" verb.
*He **never** arrives at work late.*
*He is **always** on time.*

B Write true sentences about your country's holiday customs by using the adverbs of frequency.

1 always: *Muslims always fast during the daylight hours from dawn to sunset during Ramadan.*

2 usually:

3 often:

4 sometimes:

5 not often:

6 never:

Expressing Feelings and the Causes of Feelings When describing a holiday or a special occasion, you should tell the listeners how you felt on that day. You should also talk about the activities that made you feel that way. To do this, you must know the distinction between -ed and -ing adjectives.

Language Patterns

A Let's learn about -ed and -ing adjectives.

-ed (your feeling)	-ing (makes you feel)
I'm **excited** to go home for Christmas.	Going home for Christmas is **exciting**.
Julian is **interested** in learning about Japanese wedding ceremonies.	Julian thinks Japanese wedding ceremonies are **interesting**.
Chang became **annoyed** by his uncle's comments during Thanksgiving dinner.	Chang's uncle's comments during Thanksgiving dinner were **annoying**.
Chen and Maria were **bored** because they stayed home during the Lunar New Year holiday.	Staying home during the Lunar New Year holiday was **boring** for Chen and Maria.

B **Pair work** | Ask your partner for information by using the -ed and -ing adjectives in the table. You can ask for information by using an adjective you wrote.

When do you feel...	interested excited bored amused tired frightened thrilled embarrassed ( )
Name something that you think is...	interesting exciting boring amusing tiring frightening thrilling embarrassing ( )

A When do you feel interested?
B I feel interested when I'm discussing Major League Baseball with my friends.
A Name something that you think is boring.
B Politics is very boring.

Pronunciation ◀))

A Read and listen to the sentences below. Then practice the common reductions of *him* and *her*.

when written	when spoken
A Have you seen Peter recently?	A Have you seen Peter recently?
B No, I haven't seen **him** for a while.	B No, I haven't seen-**im** for a while.
A How about Julia?	A How about Julia?
B I saw **her** during Christmas break.	B I saw-**er** during Christmas break.

B Listen and practice the conversation. Be careful when pronouncing the words *him* and *her*.

A Are you going to see Jung soon?
B Yes, I'm going to have **him** over for Thanksgiving dinner next week.
A Have you met his girlfriend yet?
B Not yet. But I'm looking forward to meeting **her**.

My Holiday Traditions When describing a holiday or a special occasion for a group, you can include the traditions you and your family follow at that time of the year. Some people prefer to visit their families and to participate in old family traditions. Others prefer to create their own new traditions.

Reading ◀◉

A   Read about the following people's holiday traditions.

I love Christmastime. One of the reasons I love Christmas is that my father decorates the outside of our house so wonderfully with Christmas lights. He really goes all out for the holidays. He puts lights in the trees in our front yard and on the front of our house. He even climbs up a ladder to hang lights from the roof! When he's done, it looks so beautiful. On Christmas Eve, my mother, father, sister, and I sit around the Christmas tree in our living room and drink eggnog. My father sometimes plays Christmas songs on the piano while my mother sings. She has a beautiful voice. For me, it's the best day of the year!

- Tricia / 22

I really like Thanksgiving because I get to see two of my closest friends in the world, Cindy and Daniel. I always spend Thanksgiving with them. A lot of people go home for the holidays, but I live too far away from my family, so Cindy and Daniel invite me to their place for the holiday. The three of us are friends from college. They're married now, but they still invite me over for Thanksgiving each year. We eat, drink, and talk about the old days. We tell funny stories about when we were in college, and then Cindy brings out the most amazing turkey you've ever seen. After dinner, I get to eat my favorite food in the whole wide world, pumpkin pie!

- Jim / 29

Following the Reading   Answer the questions.

1 What does Tricia's father do to the yard and house that she enjoys a lot?

2 What does Tricia think about the outside of her house at Christmastime?

3 What do Tricia's parents sometimes do on Christmas Eve?

4 Who does Jim usually spend the Thanksgiving holiday with?

5 How does Jim know the couple?

6 What does Jim like about the Thanksgiving holiday?

B   **Pair work** | Tell a classmate how you spend Thanksgiving and Christmas. Where do you go? What do you do? Who do you spend the most time with during these holidays?

Opener: Grabbing the Audience's Attention I When giving a speech, it is important to begin the speech by grabbing the audience's attention. Below are three attention-getting opener strategies you can use in order to grab the audience's attention and begin the speech in an interesting way.

A Read the attention-getting opener examples and write the letters in the correct columns.

1. Tell a story.	2. Use a quotation from a famous person.	3. Ask a rhetorical question.

a. Washington Irving said, "Christmas is the season for kindling the fire of hospitality."

b. The best New Year's my family ever had was January 1st, 2015. Instead of spending the day in cold Toronto, we were on the beautiful Hawaiian Island of Kauai. And rather than seeing pine trees everywhere, we were surrounded by beautiful palm trees.

c. What can get children and adults alike to dress up for the evening like their favorite comic book character? That's correct. It's Halloween!

d. Learn from yesterday. Live for today. Hope for tomorrow.   - Albert Einstein

e. What can bring families together and remind everyone how thankful they should be? That's right. You guessed it. It's Thanksgiving!

f. Every 4th of July, my family would go to the lake. Just after dark, the fireworks would begin. There were big ones, loud ones, and long ones that seemed to go on for minutes. The fireworks display never failed to make us smile, and I'll never forget it.

B   Look at the pictures. Then write an opener by using these strategies: tell a story, use a quotation from a famous person, and ask a rhetorical question.

Tell a personal story about Christmas.

Search the Internet for a quotation by a famous person about Thanksgiving.

Ask a rhetorical question about New Year's Day.

🖊 **Common Mistakes 1st, 2nd, and 3rd**

March 1th (incorrect)   March 1st (correct)

October 22th (incorrect)   October 22nd (correct)

December 23th (incorrect)   December 23rd (correct)

The Descriptive Speech: Holidays Now it is time for you to do it yourself! Use the information you learned in the previous sections in order to create an outline for a speech describing a holiday.

A Write an attention-getting opener for the topic "My Favorite Holiday." Think about which attention-getting opener strategy would best introduce your topic. After that, use the mind maps below to make notes for the body of your speech.

Attention-Getting Opener

What holiday do you enjoy?

Which strategy would you choose for your attention-getting opener?

☐ Tell a Story   ☐ Use a Quotation from a Famous Person   ☐ Ask a Rhetorical Question

Now, write your attention-getting opener.

Date and Customs

How I feel during the holiday

Why I like it

B Give a short speech describing a holiday. Use your notes from A.

> ### Introduction
> Attention-Getting Opener + Preview of Main Points
> The first Easter I can remember was when I was five years old.
> My parents told me that... Today, I'm going to tell you
> a bit about Easter. Then, I'll talk about how I feel during
> the holiday. Finally, I'll tell you why I like it.

> ### Body
> First, let's talk about Easter...

> ### Conclusion
> Summary of Main Points + Concluding Remarks
> Today, I told you a bit about Easter, how I feel during
> the holiday, and why I like it. Easter is my favorite holiday of the
> year, and I always look forward to it. Most importantly,
> it's a day to spend time with family and friends. I hope your
> next Easter is a happy one!

Checklist

1 Do adverbs of frequency come before or after main verbs? How about the "be" verb?
2 What does an adjective ending in *-ed* reveal? How about an adjective ending in *-ing*?
3 What important thing must you do at the beginning of any speech?
4 What three attention-getting opener strategies are mentioned in the unit?

Presentation Tips

Writing a Strong Conclusion

It is important to write a strong conclusion. In order to do this, you must first summarize the main points of the body. Then, you must finish the speech with memorable concluding remarks. Your last words to the audience should be thoughtful and powerful. This will leave the audience with a positive lasting impression of your talk. Here are two strategies you can use in order to make your concluding remarks memorable:

1. Make a prediction.
I am sure you will be thinking of your loved ones as you spend time with them this Christmas.

2. A Call to Action
Don't take your family for granted this holiday season. Be sure to make plans to visit them. Remember that family is the most important thing in life.

Food and Drinks

Warm-up

Look at the pictures and write the correct job title next to each person's name. Then write the first letter of each person's name in the box by the picture of the food or drink item that relates to his or her job.

baker	barista	bartender	chef

1 Catrina

2 Kevin

3 Sam

4 Yaerin

a

b

c

d

e

f

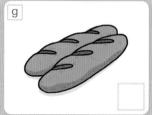

g

h

Giving Clear Instructions When describing a particular process, you should be clear with the verbs you use. There are verb groupings that are commonly used for cooking, baking, and other similar activities. Be sure that you have studied the correct verb groupings for the process you are describing.

Vocabulary

A   Complete the sentences below the pictures by using the verbs in the word box. Then put them in the correct order.

Add	Eat	Chop up	Put in	Read	Serve

1. _____ the vegetables _____ a large pot on the stove.

2. _____ the recipe.

3. _____ some vegetables.

4. _____ the soup.

5. _____ the soup with your family or friends.

6. _____ seasonings to the soup.

B   **Pair work** | Find a recipe for your favorite dish on the Internet. Then share it with a partner.

Grammar

A   Let's learn about imperatives.

Pronoun is implied but not used.	Verb (imperative) + Object/s
(You)	**Put** the rice **in** the bowl. **Chop up** the fruit and vegetables. **Don't pour** any juice down the sink. **Buy** the ingredients at the store.

B   Use imperatives to make sentences about the pictures.

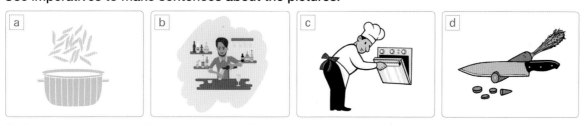

Boil some water in a pot. Put some pasta in the pot.

Using Ordinal Numbers and Sequence Adverbs When describing a process, you should use sequence words, so your audience knows in which order the steps in the process are happening. If there are many steps in the process, you should use ordinal numbers. For fewer than five steps, you can use sequence adverbs.

Language Patterns

A Let's learn about ordinal numbers and sequence adverbs.

Ordinal Numbers					Sequence Adverbs			
First	Second	Third	Fourth	Fifth	First/Firstly	Next	After that	Then
Firstly	Secondly	Thirdly	Fourthly	Fifthly	Last/Lastly/Finally			

B **Pair work** | Look at the picture about how to make different kinds of coffee drinks. Then ask your partner which drink he or she would like to learn how to make. Use ordinal numbers or sequence adverbs to describe the process to your partner. Use the verbs below.

Café Menu

Espresso	$3.50
Mocha Latte	$4.50
Café Latte	$4.00
Cappuccino	$4.00

*Helpful Verbs: pour, add, stir, serve

Pronunciation 🔊

A Read and listen to the sentences below. Then practice the common reductions of *want to*, *going to*, and *got to*.

when written	when spoken
I **want to** make a sandwich.	I **wanna** make a sandwich.
I'm **going to** cook some spaghetti.	I'm **gonna** cook some spaghetti.
I've **got to** go to the store.	I've **gotta** go to the store.

B Listen and practice. Be careful when pronouncing the words *want to*, *going to*, and *got to*.

1 Mary-Anne and I **want to** make dinner for you.

2 We were **going to** order a pizza, but we decided to make some soup instead.

3 You've **got to** add more salt to the stew. It's really bland.

Why I Like Making It / Why I Like It If your food or drink is something you enjoy making, talk about why you like making it. If it is something you enjoy eating or drinking, talk about why you like it. This will help personalize your speech and make it more interesting.

Reading 🔊

Read about the food or drinks that the people enjoy making or consuming.

I started drinking coffee when I was a freshman in university. Of course, I didn't have any money then, so the coffee I drank wasn't very good. Now I'm really into coffee. I like making espresso at home with my new espresso machine. I really love the smell of the coffee grounds. I don't drink alcohol, and I don't smoke cigarettes. But I'm definitely a coffee addict!

- Simone

I love baking! It's been my hobby for about five years now. My mother never baked when I was growing up, so I didn't learn how to do it. But I've always liked watching baking shows on television. About five years ago, I took a baking class at my local community center. Now I bake muffins, cakes, and pies for my husband and children almost every weekend. It's so much fun!

- Pauline

I enjoy good beer. I don't go out often, but when I do, I like to enjoy the delicious taste of a nice craft beer. There is a bar in my neighborhood that brews its own beer. It has a wonderful dark lager that is probably my favorite beer in the whole world. I like going to this bar, talking with my friends, and sipping a cold beer after a long workweek. It's so relaxing and fun.

- Pat

Following the Reading Answer the questions.

1 When did Simone start drinking coffee?

2 What did Simone recently purchase?

3 How long has Pauline been baking?

4 How did Pauline learn to bake?

5 What kind of beer does Pat enjoy?

6 Why does Pat like going to his local bar?

Opener: Grabbing the Audience's Attention II As mentioned in Unit 4, it is important to begin a speech by grabbing the audience's attention. Here are three more strategies you can use in order to grab the audience's attention.

A Read the additional attention-getting opener examples.

1 Start your speech by stating a shocking fact or statistic.

More than ten billion donuts are made in the USA each year.

The oldest known recipe for apple strudel was written in 1697 and is kept in a library in Vienna, Austria.

The oldest bread oven ever discovered was found in Croatia and is thought to be 6,500 years old.

2 Use an image.

Here is a picture of my grandmother's famous cinnamon buns. Today, I'm going to tell you how to make them!

3 Use a gimmick, a prop, or a visual aid.

You might want to use a gimmick, a prop, or some other visual aid. An example of a gimmick would be to put some flour on your face before your speech about baking. You could then wipe the flour from your face and say, "Oh, I'm sorry. I was just baking some bread..." There are millions of gimmicks you could use, so be creative. A prop or a visual aid is also helpful. When giving a speech about how to make cupcakes, why not bring in a batch? You could even give the audience a taste after the speech!

I made these cupcakes last night. Aren't they beautiful?

B   Create attention-getting openers for each of the topics below by using the strategies introduced on the previous page. Use the Internet if necessary for research.

1 | Start your speech by stating a shocking fact or statistic.

Use the Internet to find a shocking statistic related to coffee in your country. Write the information in your own words.

_____

2 | Use an Image.

Choose a dish you know how to make. Then find an image of it online by using your smartphone. Write a short comment to go along with your photo and introduce your topic to a partner.

This is a photo of...

_____

3 | Use a gimmick, a prop, or a visual aid.

Think of a food or a drink you would like to describe to the class. Write about a gimmick, a prop, or a visual aid that would introduce your topic to the class in an interesting way. Write a short description of your idea.

_____

Ⓥ **Common Mistakes some vs. any**

We need **any** eggs. (incorrect)   We need **some** eggs. (correct)

We don't need **some** eggs. (incorrect)   We don't need **any** eggs. (correct)

Do we need **some** eggs? (incorrect)   Do we need **any** eggs? (correct)

The Descriptive Speech: Food or Drinks Now it is time for you to do it yourself! Use the information you learned in the previous sections in order to create an outline for a speech describing a food or drink.

A Write an attention-getting opener for the topic "My Favorite Food or Drink." Think about which attention-getting opener strategy would best introduce your topic. After that, jot down some notes about your favorite food or drink to create the body of your speech.

Attention-Getting Opener

What food or drink do you enjoy?

Which strategy would you choose for your attention-getting opener?

☐ Tell a Story   ☐ Use a Quotation from a Famous Person   ☐ Ask a Rhetorical Question
☐ State a Shocking Fact or Statistic   ☐ Use an Image   ☐ Use a Gimmick, a Prop, or a Visual Aid

Now, write your attention-getting opener.

Ingredients Needed to Make It
✔
✔
✔
✔

How to Make It
✔
✔
✔
✔

Why I Like Making It / Why I Like It
✔
✔
✔
✔

B   Give a short speech about your favorite food or drink. Use your notes from A.

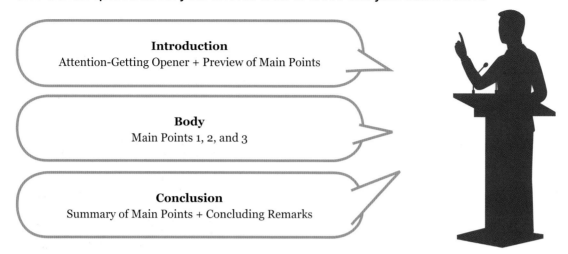

Introduction
Attention-Getting Opener + Preview of Main Points

Body
Main Points 1, 2, and 3

Conclusion
Summary of Main Points + Concluding Remarks

Checklist

1   What kinds of words should you be clear about using when describing a process?
2   Why do we use sequence words when describing processes?
3   Why is it helpful to talk about your enjoyment of the topic?
4   Give three more examples of attention-getting opener strategies.

Presentation Tips

Using Transitions

Transitions are an important part of a speech. They are signals or signposts that tell the audience you are moving from one part of the speech to the next. Transitions are especially important for the body of the speech. If your speech has three main points, you need to clearly signal to the audience that you have finished talking about main point 1 and are now moving on to main point 2. If you are giving a speech about how to make pancakes, the transition from main point 1 to main point 2 might look something like this:

I have finished talking about the ingredients needed to make pancakes. Now, I will tell you how to make pancakes.

This transition is called the "Review/Preview." Notice how the speaker has reviewed main point 1 one last time and previewed the topic of main point 2. This lets the audience know that you are moving on to your second main point. They know what the main points of the speech are because you previewed all three of the main points at the end of the introduction.

Sports and Exercise

Warm-up

Check the activities you can do or play.

Sports and Exercise Equipment When describing a sport or exercise to an audience, it is a good idea to include a list of the items one needs to participate in it. Audience members might find it helpful to know some of the key items that are required to safely and satisfyingly take part in it.

Vocabulary

A Look at the drawing and write the numbers in the correct boxes.

1 barbell	11 volleyball
2 tennis racket	12 trophy
3 basketball	13 flippers
4 basketball hoop	14 goggles
5 snorkel	15 American football
6 baseball bat	16 golf club
7 bowling ball	17 jump rope
8 bicycle	18 soccer ball
9 running shoes	19 soccer cleats
10 ping-pong paddle	20 badminton racket

B **Pair work** | Ask your partner what his or her favorite sport or exercise is. Then ask your partner what items you need to do that activity.

Grammar

A Let's learn about *must*, *must not*, *have to*, and *don't have to*.

must & must not/mustn't	have to & don't have to
In soccer, you **must not** touch the ball with your hands. You **must** kick the ball with your foot. In tennis, you **must** hit the ball within the lines. You **must not** touch the net with your racket.	In golf, you **have to** hit the ball with your club. You **don't have to** wear a hat on the golf course, but you can wear a hat if you want to. In basketball, you **have to** have five people to make a team. You **don't have to** arrive early at basketball practice, but it's a good idea to stretch before practicing.

B Complete the sentences with *must*, *mustn't*, *have to*, or *don't have to*.

1 You _____ wear a helmet if you want to play American football.

2 You _____ go snorkeling in areas where there are lots of sharks.

3 The players on a baseball team _____ wear a uniform.

4 You _____ wear running shoes. You can run barefoot if you want to.

5 You _____ surf here. The waves are too dangerous.

6 You _____ play basketball in a gym. You can play at the park, too.

What Are the Benefits? When telling an audience about an activity, it is important to use the correct verb collocation. You should also include some of the benefits of doing an activity and why you personally enjoy doing it.

Language Patterns

A Let's learn about *do*, *go*, and *play*.

do	go	play
yoga	surfing	basketball
aerobics	skiing	soccer
karate	inline-skating	American football
taekwondo	snorkeling	baseball
Pilates	cycling	tennis
judo	running	badminton

B **Pair work** | Find three classmates who can say yes to your questions regarding the activities in A. Then ask two follow-up questions to get more information from them.

Do you like to _____?	Student's Name	What are the benefits?	Why do you like it?

A Do you like to go running?

B Yes, I do.

A What are the benefits?

B It can help you increase your overall endurance and strength.

A Why do you like it?

B I love to go running because it relaxes me. It also makes me feel…

Pronunciation 🔊

A Read and listen to the words below. Then practice the pronunciations of the /θ/ and /ð/ sounds.

/θ/ (unvoiced)		/ð/ (voiced)	
thick	mara**th**on	**th**ere	ano**th**er
thin	fif**th**	**th**e	ga**th**er
thing	wi**th**	**th**is	ei**th**er

B Listen and practice. Be careful when pronouncing the /θ/ and /ð/ sounds.

1 Practice **th**ese poses ei**th**er wi**th** a friend or by yourself.

2 Ga**th**er your shoes and your ball and meet us **th**ere.

3 E**th**an ran a mara**th**on wi**th** his father and his bro**th**er.

Where to Do an Activity and Why When describing a favorite activity to an audience, you can include where you like to do it and why you like doing it there. People might be interested in trying an activity but do not know how or where to start. This information could be very helpful to them and get them started.

Reading 🔊

A Read about the kinds of sports and exercise.

I'm Pedro, and I do aerobics three times a week to stay in shape. The best place to do it is at the studio in my neighborhood. My friends asked me why I pay money to take an aerobics class when I could do it at home for free. There are a lot of free workouts on the Internet. But I like paying $100 per month because it makes me feel like I have to go. If I don't go, then I'm just throwing my money away. The studio is also large and has a nice floor, so I think it's better at the studio.

I'm Stephanie, and I love two things: going to the beach and playing badminton. I think the beach is the best place to play badminton because you don't have to wear shoes and you can enjoy the wonderful breeze from the ocean. I usually play badminton with my husband, Ralph. He also likes playing badminton at the beach. Some people look at us strangely because they wonder how we can play without a net. But we don't care. We just have fun hitting the shuttlecock back and forth. We don't even keep score!

Following the Reading Answer the questions.

1 How often does Pedro do aerobics?

2 Why does Pedro pay money to take an aerobics class?

3 What does Pedro think about the studio?

4 What are Stephanie's two favorite activities?

5 What doesn't Stephanie have to wear when she plays badminton at the beach?

6 How do people look at Stephanie and her husband when they play badminton at the beach?

B Where is the best place to exercise in your neighborhood? And why is it a good place to work out?

The local fitness center is the best place to exercise in my neighborhood. It has a lot of exercise equipment. And the monthly fee is reasonable.

Using PowerPoint Slides: Dos Visual aids can enhance the quality of a speech, however, the misuse of this technology can have the opposite effect. We must understand that the purpose of using PowerPoint slides is to support the information in a speech, not to replace it. Here are some things to remember.

A Match the headlines to the correct examples. Then check the good examples.

> Clearly Contrast Your Text and Background Colors
> Use Bullet Points & Limit the Amount of Text
> Use Good-Quality Graphics and Images

1 _____

a

Taekwondo

- punch & kick
- self-defense
- get in shape
- increase your flexibility
- learn self-discipline

☐

b

Taekwondo has several benefits. You can learn how to punch and kick effectively. You can also learn how to defend yourself in a fight. Taekwondo helps you get in shape and increase your flexibility. It teaches you self-discipline. Overall, it is a very useful activity.

☐

2 _____

a

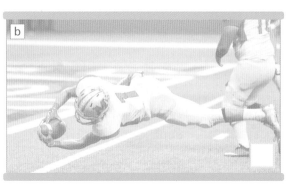

b

3 _____

a

Pilates

- get stronger
- become more flexible
- lose weight
- get in shape

☐

b

Pilates

- get stronger
- become more flexible
- lose weight
- get in shape

☐

B Choose one of the PowerPoint presentations below and give the body portion of the speech to a partner by using the slides.

1 How to Run a Marathon

Running a Marathon

Items Needed to Run a Marathon

- good shoes & socks
- light shorts & light shirt
- hat, sunscreen, fitness tracker, hip pack

Benefits

- increase endurance
- build strength and lose weight
- reduce stress

The Best Place to Run a Marathon and Why

- run outside
- see nature
- fresh air and nature inspires you

Firstly, I'd like to tell you what you need to run a marathon. You must wear comfortable shoes and socks. You also have to...

2 How to Do Yoga

Doing Yoga

Items Needed to Do Yoga

- mat & water bottle
- comfortable clothes
- spacious area

Benefits

- increase flexibility
- build muscle and lose weight
- relax your body and mind

The Best Place to Do Yoga and Why

- studio
- lots of space
- teacher can help you

I have told you about the benefits of doing yoga. Now, I'll tell you about the best place to do yoga and why. Although I pay more than one hundred dollars a month to study yoga in a studio, it is totally worth the money...

🖐 Common Mistakes Numbers

one hundred (correct)   a hundred (correct)   one a hundred (incorrect)

The Descriptive Speech: Sports and Exercise Now it is time for you to do it yourself! Use the information you learned in the previous sections in order to create an outline for a speech describing a sport or exercise.

A Write an attention-getting opener for the topic "My Favorite Sport or Exercise." Think about which attention-getting opener strategy would best introduce your topic. After that, use the notepads below to do a free-writing session in order to create the body of your speech.

Attention-Getting Opener

What sport or exercise do you enjoy?

Which strategy would you choose for your attention-getting opener?

☐ Tell a Story ☐ Use a Quotation from a Famous Person ☐ Ask a Rhetorical Question

☐ State a Shocking Fact or Statistic ☐ Use an Image ☐ Use a Gimmick, a Prop, or a Visual Aid

Now, write your attention-getting opener.

B Give a short speech about how to do a sport or exercise. Use your notes from A.

> **Introduction**
> Attention-Getting Opener + Preview of Main Points

> **Body**
> Main Points 1, 2, and 3
> (Use transitions to move from main point 1 to 2 and from 2 to 3.)
> I have talked about the items needed to play basketball. Now,
> I will talk about the benefits of playing basketball...

> **Conclusion**
> Summary of Main Points + Concluding Remarks

Checklist

1 What kind of list should you include when describing a sport or exercise?
2 What is the difference between "must not" and "don't have to"?
3 What verb collocations do we use for the following activities: basketball, Pilates, and skiing?
4 What is the purpose of using visual aids such as PowerPoint?
5 What three tips are given regarding the use of PowerPoint slides in a presentation?

Presentation Tips

Organizational Patterns in the Body of the Speech

There are a number of ways we can organize the body of a speech. If you were giving a speech about how to put together a ping-pong table, you might want to use a **time** organizing pattern. A time organizing pattern describes a process chronologically.

Another organizing pattern is the **past, present, and future** pattern. In a speech about weightlifting, you might want to talk about weightlifting in the 1960s and 70s, weightlifting today, and what you think weightlifting will be like in the future.

The last organizing pattern I'd like to discuss is the **related subtopics** pattern. In a speech about aerobics videos, the speaker could talk about aerobics DVDs, online aerobics videos, and virtual reality aerobics videos.

Natural Processes

Warm-up

Fill in the blanks with the correct words from the word box.

adolescent	adult	butterfly	caterpillar	child	egg	flower
	fruit	infant	pupa	seeds	child	tree

Life Cycle of an Apple Tree

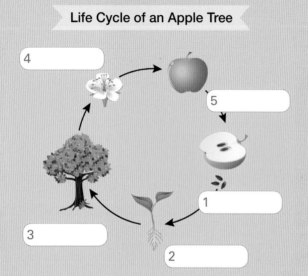

4 _____

5 _____

1 _____

2 _____

3 _____

Life Cycle of a Butterfly

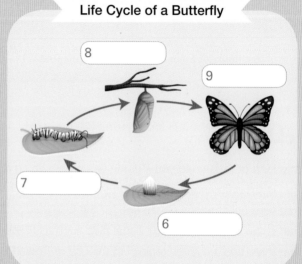

8 _____

9 _____

7 _____

6 _____

Life Cycle of a Human

10 _____

11 _____

12 _____

13 _____

Life Cycles Natural processes often involve living organisms that go through different stages of development. Together, these stages make up the life cycle of an organism. When choosing a topic for a speech explaining a natural process, an explanation of a life cycle is a good choice.

Vocabulary

A Match the words with the correct definitions.

offspring	pupa/chrysalis	siblings	reproduce	life cycle	seed

1 _____ : a kernel or pit capable of growing into a plant

2 _____ : the changes an organism goes through during its life

3 _____ : the shell or cocoon that a butterfly emerges from when it is fully grown

4 _____ : to make a copy of; to produce another organism

5 _____ : the child or children of parents

6 _____ : brothers or sisters

B **Class activity** | Change the sentences in the left column into questions in the right column. Then find someone who can say yes to the questions and ask for follow-up information.

	Find someone who...	Questions
1	has raised a pet that has had offspring.	*Have you ever had a pet that has had offspring?*
2	has experienced a natural disaster.	
3	has planted a flower, a tree, or a vegetable.	
4	has spent winter or summer in another country.	

A Have you ever had a pet that has had offspring?

B Yes, I have.

A How many offspring did your pet have?

B My dog had one litter of six puppies.

Grammar

A Let's learn about the present perfect tense.

have + (past participle)

George **has grown** his own fruit and vegetables for years.
Jimin **has grown up** a lot since the last time I saw her.
Have Artemis and Nathanial **raised** chickens on their farm for three years?
We **haven't eaten** the apples our neighbors gave us yet.

B Complete the sentences with the correct usage of the present perfect tense.

1 _____ you _____ the sapling in the yard? It's growing really fast. (see)

2 Joe and Chang _____ camping yet this year. (not / be)

3 I _____ care of fish for several years. (take)

4 _____ you _____ ducks on your farm? (raise)

The Stages of Growth in a Life Cycle When describing stages of development, it is helpful to know some of the verbs that explain a growth process. They can help you describe a growth cycle in a clear and understandable way.

Language Patterns

A Let's learn some expressions for describing the stages in a process.

Beginning Stages	Middle Stages	Final Stages
begins... starts... originates...	develops into... grows into... turns into... changes into...	becomes... grows up to become... ultimately becomes...

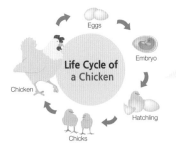

First, a chicken **begins** its life as an egg. Next, it **develops into** an embryo. Then, it **grows into** a hatchling. After that, it **turns into** a chick. Finally, it **becomes** a chicken.

B Choose one of the pictures and describe the life cycle by using the vocabulary from A.

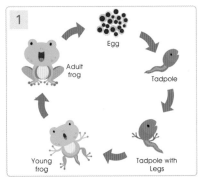
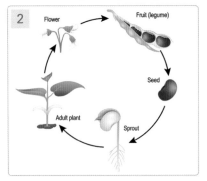

Pronunciation 🔊

A Read and listen to the words below. Then practice the pronunciations of the /l/ and /r/ sounds.

/l/		/r/	
legs	lake	fruit	flower
flower	lizard	frog	sprout

B Listen and practice the sentences. Be careful when pronouncing the /l/ and /r/ sounds.

1 The tadpole in the lake has grown legs.

2 The red flower has sprouted from the ground.

3 The lemons have been picked from the tree.

The Positives and Negatives of a Natural Process When giving a speech about a natural process, you should give your opinions regarding the good or bad results of that process because it will give the audience a better understanding of the topic.

Reading 🔊

A Read about the different examples of natural processes.

There were several ups and downs during my pregnancy. In the beginning, I got really bad morning sickness. Everything that I ate made me feel really sick. My back also hurt because I gained a lot of weight. But there were some good things, too. First, my husband did everything for me. He did all of the grocery shopping and the cleaning. My skin also looked really good. Of course, the best part of the pregnancy was the day I got to hold my beautiful baby!

- Sarah

Hurricane Rita hit our city five years ago. Unfortunately, our garage was damaged when a tree fell on it. My wife's car also got scratched by the branches of the tree. Luckily, my car was not damaged at all. In addition, about an hour before the hurricane hit the city, our cat ran away. We looked for her, but we couldn't find her. Fortunately, she returned the day after the hurricane. She must have known a hurricane was coming and hid somewhere safe.

- Richard

I really love when winter changes into spring. There are a couple of reasons why I love spring. First, spring is warm and sunny. It is also the time of year when we can see beautiful cherry blossoms. Cherry blossoms only bloom once a year for a few weeks in spring. I really hate winter for several reasons. First, it is cold and dark during winter. Second, I feel depressed in winter because I can't go outside and do anything fun or interesting.

- Yuki

Following the Reading Read the sentences and mark them True or False.

1 Sarah got bad morning sickness at the end of her pregnancy.　　[True / False]

2 A benefit of Sarah's pregnancy was that her husband did all the chores.　[True / False]

3 Richard's living room was damaged during the hurricane.　　[True / False]

4 Richard's family's cat ran away after the hurricane.　　[True / False]

5 Yuki loves when cherry blossoms bloom in spring.　　[True / False]

6 Yuki feels depressed in winter because she can't go outside.　　[True / False]

B Which season do you enjoy the most and why?

I love spring. I feel so hopeful when the snow begins to melt and the leaves on the trees begin to grow.

Using PowerPoint Slides: Don'ts We must resist certain bad habits when using PowerPoint slides in a speech. The improper use of slides can actually diminish the quality of a speech instead of enhancing it. Here are a number of things a speaker should not do when using PowerPoint slides during a presentation.

A Read the advice about creating PowerPoint slides and then choose the pictures that match the advice given.

1 **Don't use more than six bullet points for one slide.**

You don't want to give the audience too many bullet points to look at in each slide. Instead of using more than six bullet points, it is better to create another slide.

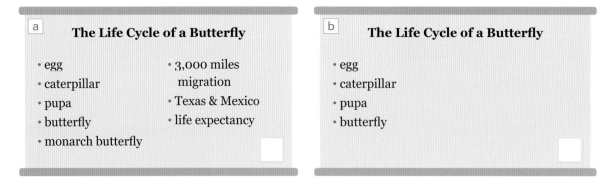

2 **Don't read your slides.**

Do not read the information exactly as it is written on the slide. Instead, use the slides as an outline for your speech. Speak conversationally as you cover each bullet point. This will give the audience the impression that you know the material well.

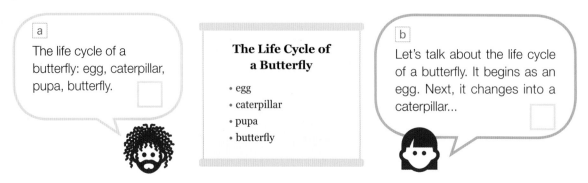

3 **Don't change the background color template for each slide.**

You should be the focus of your speech or presentation, not your PowerPoint slides. Distracting color changes or images will pull attention away from you and toward the slides.

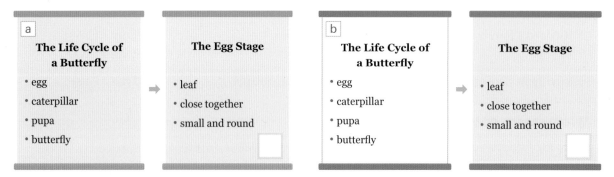

B **Fill in the blanks.**

1 Look at the diagram and complete the PowerPoint slide with the correct information.

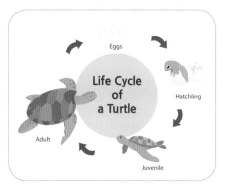

The Life Cycle of a Turtle

a _____

b _____

c _____

d _____

2 Read the part of the speech and complete the PowerPoint slide with the correct information.

The Stages of Human Development

a _____

b _____

c _____

d _____

I would like to describe for you the four stages of human development. First, we begin life in infancy. We then enter into childhood at the age of two. After that, we grow into adolescence at about the age of 12. At around the age of 19, we become adults. This stage is called adulthood. These are the four stages of human development.

3 Fill in the blanks in the dialogue by using the information in the PowerPoint slide.

The Growth of a Pumpkin

• a seed
• a sprout
• a plant with vines
• flowers
• green pumpkins
• fully grown pumpkins

Let's talk about the growth of a pumpkin. A pumpkin ᵃ_____ its life as ᵇ_____. Next, the seed ᶜ_____ a sprout. After that, it changes into ᵈ_____ with ᵉ_____. Then, ᶠ_____ grow on the vines. The flowers ᵍ_____ green pumpkins. Finally, the green pumpkins ʰ_____ fully grown ⁱ_____.

🌱 **Common Mistakes a/an**

an sprout (incorrect)   a hour (incorrect)   a plants (incorrect)

a sprout (correct)   an hour (correct)   plants (correct)

The Informative Speech: Natural Processes Now it is time for you to do it yourself! Use the information you learned in the previous sections in order to create an outline for a speech explaining a natural process.

A Write an attention-getting opener for the topic "Natural Processes." Think about which attention-getting opener strategy would best introduce your topic. Refer to the example PowerPoint slides and then create your own in order to outline your speech.

Attention-Getting Opener

Which natural process would you like to explain to the class in a short speech?

Which strategy would you choose for your attention-getting opener?

☐ Tell a Story ☐ Use a Quotation from a Famous Person ☐ Ask a Rhetorical Question
☐ State a Shocking Fact or Statistic ☐ Use an Image ☐ Use a Gimmick, a Prop, or a Visual Aid

Now, write your attention-getting opener.

The Life Cycle of a Chicken

The Life Cycle

- egg
- embryo
- hatchling
- chick
- chicken

The Positives

- gives us eggs
- meat provides us with protein
- chickens eat insects

The Negatives

- bad farms
- small cages
- too many antibiotics

Conclusion

We should respect the chicken because it has given us a lot!

Have you ever held a chicken? I have. My uncle raised chickens on his farm, so we went there often when I was young. It was really fun. Today, I will tell you about the life cycle of a chicken and...

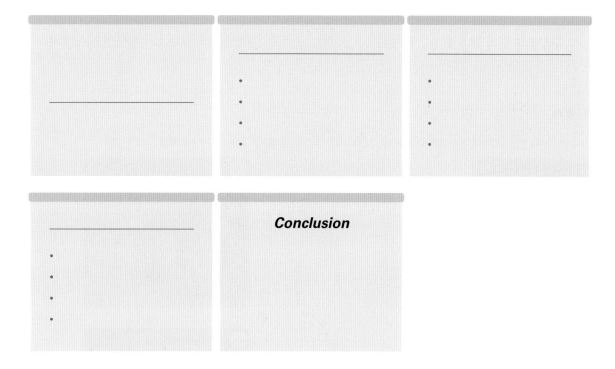

Conclusion

B   Give a short speech about a natural process. Use your notes from A.

Checklist

1   What do we call the natural stages a living organism goes through?
2   What kinds of verbs or phrases can we use to describe a cycle or process?
3   Why should speakers include the positives and negatives of a natural process?
4   What are the three don'ts given in the unit regarding the use of PowerPoint slides in presentations?
5   What can the improper use of PowerPoint slides do to the quality of a speech?

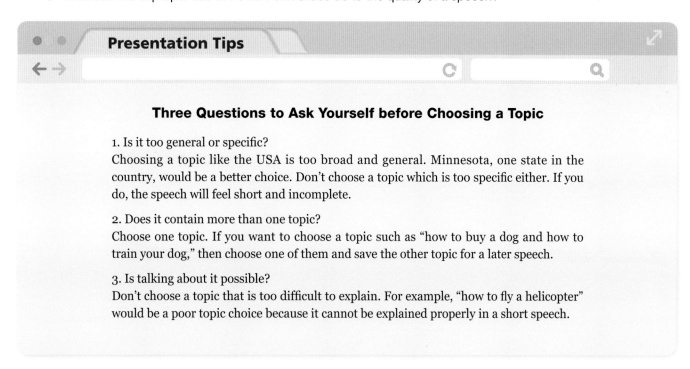

Presentation Tips

Three Questions to Ask Yourself before Choosing a Topic

1. Is it too general or specific?
Choosing a topic like the USA is too broad and general. Minnesota, one state in the country, would be a better choice. Don't choose a topic which is too specific either. If you do, the speech will feel short and incomplete.

2. Does it contain more than one topic?
Choose one topic. If you want to choose a topic such as "how to buy a dog and how to train your dog," then choose one of them and save the other topic for a later speech.

3. Is talking about it possible?
Don't choose a topic that is too difficult to explain. For example, "how to fly a helicopter" would be a poor topic choice because it cannot be explained properly in a short speech.

Manmade Processes or Inventions

Warm-up

A Match the first stages in the processes with their final stages by connecting the dots.

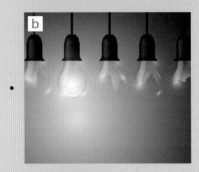

B What are some other manmade processes or inventions that have made your life better?

Inventors and Inventions When giving a speech about a manmade process or invention, you might want to include information about the person or people responsible for creating the process or invention.

Vocabulary

A   Complete the sentences with the correct words from the word box.

designed	discovered	experiments	gadget	imagine	important

1   Marie Curie _____ radium on December 21, 1898.

2   When Alexander Fleming discovered penicillin, it was an _____ discovery for medical science.

3   The Tesla automobile was _____ by Elon Musk and his team of engineers.

4   "_____" is another word for "device."

5   Scientists often conduct _____ in their laboratories.

6   Inventors not only have the ability to _____ new inventions, but they can actually build them, too.

B   Who is your favorite inventor? What invention did that inventor make?

Grammar

A   Let's learn about the active voice and the passive voice.

Active Voice	Passive Voice
Who **invented** the light bulb? Thomas Edison **invented** the light bulb.	Who **was** the light bulb **invented by**? It **was invented by** Thomas Edison.
Who **created** the first electric battery? Allesandro Volta **created** the first electric battery.	Who **was** the first electric battery **created by**? It **was created by** Allesandro Volta.

B   **Pair work** | Match the words in the word box with the correct pictures. Then ask your partner who invented the items in the table. Have your partner answer the questions in the passive voice.

disposable diapers	fidget spinner	light bulb	Ford Model T	paper	Teflon

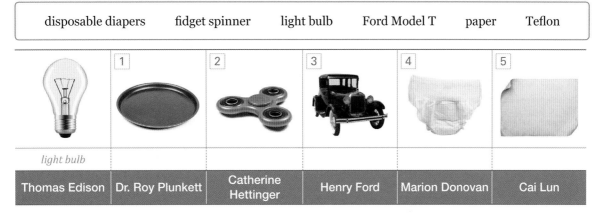

	1	2	3	4	5
light bulb					
Thomas Edison	Dr. Roy Plunkett	Catherine Hettinger	Henry Ford	Marion Donovan	Cai Lun

A   Who was the light bulb invented by?

B   It was invented by Thomas Edison.

Cause and Effect When describing the stages in a manmade process, it is helpful to explain the effects of certain processes and their causes. This way, we can see whether the results of the processes are useful and helpful to society, or if they are harmful and need to be changed.

Language Patterns

A Let's learn about cause and effect.

Cause *because, when, if, since, due to*	Effect *so, therefore, as a result, so that, then*
The inventor became rich **because** her inventions were so popular. **Since** the product didn't work very well, the company stopped making it. The crops were destroyed **due to** too much rainfall in the region.	Her inventions were popular, **so** she became rich. The product didn't work very well; **therefore**, the company stopped making it. There was too much rainfall in the region; **as a result**, the crops were destroyed.

B Read the partial sentences containing causes and effects. Then complete the sentences with logical causes for the effects and effects of the causes.

1 The businessman lost all of his money because _____.

2 _____, so the computer didn't work anymore.

3 _____; therefore, my family was very happy.

4 Since the phone allowed people to communicate across long distances, _____.

Pronunciation 🔊

A Read and listen to the words below. Then practice the common pronunciations of regular verbs in the past simple tense ending in *-ed*.

/d/	/t/	/ɪd/
allow**ed**	stopp**ed**	stat**ed**
imagin**ed**	work**ed**	invent**ed**
turn**ed**	produc**ed**	need**ed**
studi**ed**	process**ed**	collect**ed**

B Listen and practice the sentences. Be careful when pronouncing the /d/, /t/, and /ɪd/ sounds.

1 Milk is heat**ed** and then cool**ed** in order to kill harmful pathogens.

2 Bell invent**ed** the first working telephone, which was produc**ed** and us**ed** by many.

3 The company allow**ed** the product to be produc**ed** and assembl**ed** overseas.

How It Works When describing how a manmade process works, you should start at the beginning of the process and finish by discussing the last stage in the process. This will give the audience a better understanding of the overall process being described.

Reading 🔊

A Read about the inventions and innovations.

Wind power uses energy from the wind and turns it into electricity. Wind energy is made when the large blades of a windmill spin in a circle. The blades cause a large metal rod to turn. When the rod turns, a generator produces electricity. Electricity from the generator is sent to houses and businesses in the area. Wind energy is clean because it doesn't produce any smoke or harmful chemicals. Smoke and chemicals in the air can make people sick and cause long-term damage to their bodies.

Coffee production begins on coffee farms in South America and Africa. Farmers pick coffee cherries and remove the beans. The beans are then dried and roasted at high temperatures. By roasting the beans in a large oven, they become dark and hard. Then, they are ready to be sold. We can buy the beans and grind them into fresh coffee ourselves, or we can buy the coffee already ground. When hot water is added to the ground coffee, it is ready to be consumed.

Following the Reading Change the incorrect sentences into correct ones.

1 The blades of a wind turbine cause a generator to turn.

2 Wind energy is not considered clean energy.

3 Coffee comes from farms in North America and Australia.

4 Roasting the beans at high temperatures makes them soft.

B Make a list of three everyday products and then write where the raw materials for the products come from.

What?	*paper*			
Where from?	*trees*			

Using Notecards: Dos and Don'ts A 4x6 inch notecard can be a very helpful tool when giving a speech. Although we don't want to memorize or read the speech, glancing at key words and phrases on 4x6 inch notecards in order to remember key points is perfectly acceptable during a speech.

A **Match the dos and don'ts with the correct bubbles.**

> a Do underline important words and phrases.
> b Don't write messily or in small print.
> c Do number your cards.
> d Don't write out your speech word for word.
> e Do use bullet points.

The Kitchen Blender

Attention-Getting Opener: This morning, I went to my favorite smoothie shop, Juice Heaven. I ordered my usual, a mango pineapple smoothie with extra ice. It's so refreshing after my morning run. As I waited in line, I got to thinking about who invented the blender. I mean, without it, there wouldn't be any delicious smoothies.

Preview
- Stephen Poplawski
- how it works
- why I like this invention

1

1

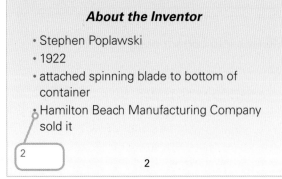

About the Inventor
- Stephen Poplawski
- 1922
- attached spinning blade to bottom of container
- Hamilton Beach Manufacturing Company sold it

2

2

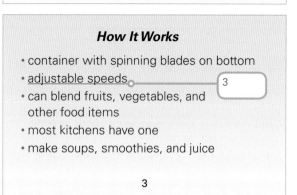

How It Works
- container with spinning blades on bottom
- adjustable speeds
- can blend fruits, vegetables, and other food items
- most kitchens have one
- make soups, smoothies, and juice

3

3

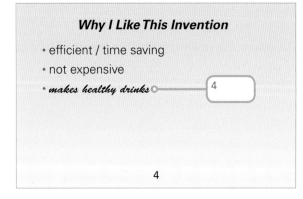

Why I Like This Invention
- efficient / time saving
- not expensive
- *makes healthy drinks*

4

4

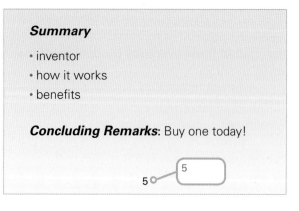

Summary
- inventor
- how it works
- benefits

Concluding Remarks: Buy one today!

5

5

B   Read the speech and then complete the notecards with information based on the talk.

Have you ever wondered how a light bulb works? Today, I'm going to talk about the inventor of the light bulb, how a light bulb works, and the benefits of the light bulb. First, let's talk about the inventor.

The light bulb was invented by Thomas Edison in the late 1800s. Edison had a laboratory in Menlo Park, New Jersey, where his team of scientists helped him improve his invention. Edison is known for bringing light into the homes of people and for changing the way we live. I have talked about Thomas Edison.

Next, I will tell you how a light bulb works. A light bulb consists of a thin piece of wire, called a filament, which sits inside of a glass bulb. When electricity passes through the filament, it begins to glow. Since the filament sits inside of a glass bulb, light shines in all directions. I have talked about how a light bulb works.

Finally, I will discuss the benefits of the light bulb. In the 1800s, households went dark in the evenings. People had oil lamps and candles, but they didn't work very well. The light bulb changed the way people lived. People were able to work later and to be more productive. They were also able to have parties that lasted all night because the rooms in their houses were well lit. I have talked about the benefits.

Now, I will summarize today's talk. Today, I discussed Thomas Edison, I talked about how the light bulb works, and I talked about how it benefitted people at the time. The next time you turn a light on in your home, I hope you will think about Thomas Edison and his invention. If you are interested in learning more about Edison, I recommend visiting the website www.thomasedison.com. Thank you.

Attention-Getting Opener:
Have you ever wondered how a light bulb works?

Preview
• [1]_____ of the light bulb
• how a light bulb works
• the [2]_____ of the light bulb

1

About the Inventor

• invented by [3]_____
• in late [4]_____
• a laboratory in [5]_____,
  [6]_____
• changed the way we live

2

How It Works
• consists of a thin piece of wire called a [7]_____
• filament sits inside [8]_____
• When electricity passes through the filament, it begins to [9]_____.
• Light shines in all [10]_____.

3

The Benefits of the Light Bulb
• 1800s, households went [11]_____
• able to work later and to be more [12]_____
• parties that lasted [13]_____

4

Summary
• Thomas Edison
• [14]_____
• how it benefitted people

Concluding Remarks:
Visit the [15]_____ www.thomasedison.com.

5

Do It Yourself

The Informative Speech: Manmade Processes or Inventions Now it is time for you to do it yourself! Use the information you learned in the previous sections in order to create an outline for a speech explaining a manmade process.

A Write an attention-getting opener for the topic "Manmade Processes or Inventions." Think about which attention-getting opener strategy would best introduce your topic. After that, write notes on the notecards to create the body of your speech.

Attention-Getting Opener

Which manmade process or invention would you like to explain to the class in a short speech?

Which strategy would you choose for your attention-getting opener?
- ☐ Tell a Story   ☐ Use a Quotation from a Famous Person   ☐ Ask a Rhetorical Question
- ☐ State a Shocking Fact or Statistic   ☐ Use an Image   ☐ Use a Gimmick, a Prop, or a Visual Aid

Now, write your attention-getting opener.

_____

Attention-Getting Opener:

Preview

- •
- •
- •

1

_____

- •
- •
- •

2

_____

- •
- •
- •
- •

3

_____

- •
- •
- •

4

Summary

- •
- •
- •

Concluding Remarks:

5

B Give a short speech about a manmade process, or an invention. Use your notes from A.

Checklist

1 When describing how an invention works, who should you mention in the speech?

2 Why should we explain the effects of a process in a speech about a manmade process?

3 Where should you start and finish when describing a process?

4 How can 4x6 inch notecards be helpful during a speech?

5 What are the dos and don'ts regarding notecards mentioned in the unit?

Presentation Tips

The Four Main Modes of Delivery

There are the four main modes of delivery in public speaking:

1. The Scripted Delivery
The scripted delivery is a speech that is read to an audience. All of the words in the speech are said exactly as they are written on the page.

2. The Memorized Delivery
The memorized delivery is similar to the scripted delivery except the speaker has memorized all of the words on the paper.

3. The Improvised Delivery
The improvised delivery is a method where the speaker has done no preparation beforehand. The entire speech is made up "on the spot."

4. The Extemporized Delivery
The extemporized delivery is the most effective method of delivery. This occurs when the speaker covers all of the essential information in the speech outline but does so in a conversational manner while maintaining good eye contact with the audience. The speech is not memorized, nor is it read to the audience.

Opinions

Warm-up

Read the opinions and then say whether you agree or disagree with them.

Traveling abroad is more enjoyable than traveling in your own country.

I disagree. I think traveling in your own country is more enjoyable than traveling abroad.

Eating out is better than eating at home. I hate doing the dishes!

Watching a movie at home is better than going to the theater.

Summer is so much better than winter. I love going to the beach.

Making Comparisons Giving a persuasive speech about why one object or method is better than another requires the ability to make comparisons. This section contains some helpful vocabulary and grammar for making comparisons between objects or methods.

Vocabulary

A Read the comments and circle the words that are the most logical.

1 Playing games on a computer is more (convenient / interesting) than playing games on a game console because you can play games and surf the Internet on the same machine.

2 I think walking to work is more (annoying / satisfying) than taking the bus because you get exercise from walking to work, and you can say hello to your neighbors in the morning.

3 Winter is less (enjoyable / depressing) than spring because it's dark and gloomy, and it's too cold to go outside.

4 Studying English in a classroom setting is more (frustrating / useful) than studying online because you have the opportunity to practice speaking English with the teacher and your classmates.

5 Taking care of dogs is more (convenient / difficult) than taking care of cats because dogs require constant attention from their owners. Cats are (satisfied / unsatisfied) even when they are alone as long as they have access to food and water.

B **Pair work** | Give your opinions about the statements in A. Then compare your opinions with a partner's opinions.

Grammar

A Let's learn about comparative adjectives.

one syllable adjectives + *r* or *er*	*more / less* + two or more syllable adjectives	two syllable adjectives ending in *y* → delete *y* and add *ier*
nice = nice**r** large = large**r** tall = tall**er** fast = fast**er** cool = cool**er**	**more** delicious **more** convenient **more** educational **less** enjoyable **less** useful	happy = happ**ier** friendly = friend**lier** funny = funn**ier** pretty = prett**ier** flashy = flash**ier**

*Irregular comparative adjectives: *good - better* & *bad - worse*

B Write true sentences by using the adjectives in the table.

1	is **larger** than
2	is **faster** than
3	is **more delicious** than
4	is **less enjoyable** than
5	is **funnier** than

Giving Your Opinion When giving a persuasive speech, it is important to use proper words and phrases for giving opinions. There are lots of different expressions you can use to give an opinion. Below are several expressions you can use during a discussion or during your persuasive speech.

Language Patterns

A   Let's learn some expressions for giving opinions.

Giving Opinions	
I (really) think that...	My personal opinion is that...
I agree with... / I disagree with...	Personally, my opinion is that...
I feel that...	In my opinion, / My opinion is...
I (strongly) believe (that)...	To be honest, / In my honest opinion,...
I'm sure that...	I would say that...

B   **Pair work** | **Make statements about the pictures. Then let your partner agree or disagree with your statements by using the expressions in A.**

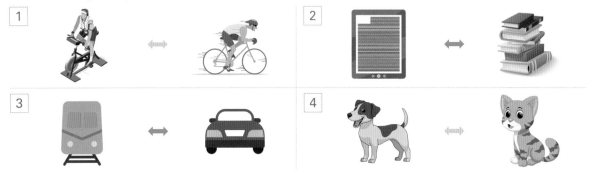

A In my opinion, riding a bike on the road is more enjoyable than riding an exercise bike in the gym because you can appreciate the scenery while riding a bike.

B Yes, I agree with you. But I would say that riding an exercise bike is more convenient. You can work out with an exercise bike indoors on a rainy day.

Pronunciation 🔊

A   Read and listen to the words below. Then practice the pronunciations of the /s/, /z/, and /ɪz/ sounds.

/s/	/z/	/ɪz/
it's	roads	touches
looks	feels	wishes
takes	seems	dances
bikes	reads	exercises
streets	sounds	mixes

B   Listen and circle the words with the different ending "s" sounds.

1 a. it's   b. streets   c. touches   4 a. needs   b. mixes   c. watches

2 a. likes   b. reads   c. rides   5 a. pats   b. barks   c. purrs

3 a. walks   b. fixes   c. bikes

Personal Experience When giving a persuasive speech, you should include strong facts and data to support your argument. However, another way to strengthen that argument is by including your own personal experience with the topic. A moving personal story can be very persuasive.

Reading 🔊

A Read about the people's preferences in each situation.

If you are going to take a long trip, I recommend riding on a bus. I like riding on buses because they move slowly, and you can appreciate the scenery as you look out the window. Noticing the small changes in the landscape is very interesting. Airplanes travel too high above the ground and move too quickly, so you can't notice the small changes in the geography. The next time you travel, you should try doing it by bus.

- Bert

I think tablets are good learning tools for children. My son likes to color on my tablet. I downloaded an app for him that lets him see the pictures in black and white. Then, by using his finger, he can color the pictures. It's more convenient than a coloring book because he doesn't need any crayons or paint. He can also easily undo any mistakes he makes by simply clicking a button. Finally, he will be more prepared for a future which will require people to be comfortable using technology.

- Jin

The robotic vacuum cleaner is better than the standard vacuum. It saves you a lot of time because you don't have to push the vacuum all around your house or apartment. When I'm at work, the robotic vacuum cleaner sucks up all the dust and dirt in my house. When I get home in the evening, I can just get some rest instead of vacuuming my floor. I still have to mop, but maybe someone will invent a robotic mop soon.

- Kim

Following the Reading Answer the questions.

1 Why does Bert like taking the bus more than flying?

2 What does Jin think about children using tablets?

3 What does Jin's son like to do on her tablet?

4 Why does Kim like the robotic vacuum cleaner?

5 What does Kim hope someone will invent in the future?

B Name an object that you use every day and cannot live without. Why do you think it is so useful?

I use my laptop every day, and I can't live without it. I talk to my friends through social networking sites, I work on my computer, and I watch television and movies on it.

Choosing a Persuasive Speech Topic Choosing a persuasive speech topic can be difficult. However, there are several questions that you can ask yourself in order to improve the likelihood that the topic you chose is a good one. If you can answer yes to the four questions, you are ready to move on.

A   Match the four questions with the correct answers in the speech balloons.

Nikki's Persuasive Claim

Bringing your own tumbler to a coffee shop is better than using a paper or plastic cup.

a Is it personal to you?
b Do you know who your audience is?
c Is what you are asking your audience to do possible?
d Is your topic interesting and controversial?

(1) Yes, it is. People are addicted to disposable coffee cups. And it certainly is more convenient to get a paper or plastic cup of coffee at a coffee shop. But by bringing our own tumblers, we can reduce millions of tons of waste. I think my topic will really challenge people's habits. ☐

(2) Yes, it is. I really care about the environment. I'm a biology major, and I realize how precious our planet is. I also want to have a family in the future. What kind of future will there be? ☐

(3) Absolutely! My audience is in university, just like me. We survive on coffee. The average university student drinks 1 to 2 cups of coffee a day. I think my topic will resonate with my class members. ☐

(4) Yes, it is. I'm not asking the audience to stop buying coffee tomorrow. I'm asking them to think about bringing their own tumblers to the coffee shop. And I'm asking them to visit a website. I'm just trying to plant seeds in their minds. ☐

B Follow these steps in order to choose a good persuasive speech topic for this unit's speech.

Step 1: Brainstorming

Complete the mind map for the following topic: *"why one object or method is better than another."* Remember that your topic should be controversial (not something everyone agrees with) and something you are passionate about. Choose topics that you would consider yourself an expert on because they have personally affected you or because you have spent a lot of time thinking about them or researching them.

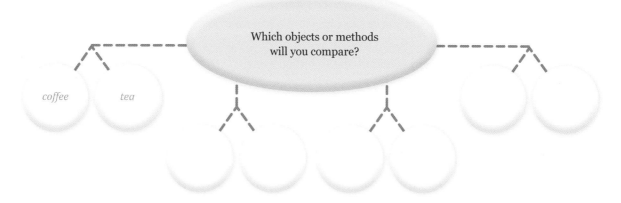

Step 2: Consider your audience.

Conduct a quick survey in order to get some feedback regarding your classmates' feelings about your topic. Tell them your persuasive claim (the main topic of your persuasive speech in one sentence; ex. bringing your own tumbler to the coffee shop is better than using a paper or plastic cup) and check their reactions to it in the table. If about half agree and half disagree, that's great. It means you've chosen a controversial topic. If everyone agrees or disagrees, then maybe your topic isn't controversial enough. If most or all of the respondents say they don't care, then you should think about changing your topic.

Your Persuasive Claim	Agree	Don't Care	Disagree
Student 1			
Student 2			
Student 3			
Student 4			
Student 5			

Step 3: Ask yourself if what you are asking of your audience is possible? `Yes` `No`

Instead of insisting that your audience give up eating meat and become vegetarian, ask them to visit a website after your talk. Getting them to visit a website or watch a video on vegetarianism or veganism is a victory when giving a short persuasive speech. You can't expect huge changes in a short time.

Step 4: Is your topic controversial? Is it persuasive? `Yes` `No`

Make sure that your topic is controversial enough. Make sure it is persuasive. The purpose of this speech is not to simply inform your audience about something. You are trying to change the way they think about a particular topic.

Do It Yourself

The Persuasive Speech: Why One Object or Method Is Better than Another Now it is time for you to do it yourself! Use the information you learned in the previous sections in order to create an outline for a speech stating why one object or method is better than another.

A Write an attention-getting opener for the topic "Why One Object or Method Is Better than Another." Think about which attention-getting opener strategy would best introduce your topic. Refer to the example PowerPoint slides and create your own in order to outline your speech.

Which two objects or methods would you like to compare? Why is one object or method better than the other?

Which strategy would you choose for your attention-getting opener?

☐ Tell a Story ☐ Use a Quotation from a Famous Person ☐ Ask a Rhetorical Question

☐ State a Shocking Fact or Statistic ☐ Use an Image ☐ Use a Gimmick, a Prop, or a Visual Aid

Now, write your attention-getting opener.

You should take the subway!

More Convenient

- no traffic
- many stations in the city
- not expensive

Better for the Environment

- less air pollution
- less noise pollution in the city

Positive Experience

- I take the subway to work every day.
- I listen to music or play phone games.

Conclusion

Make the city a nicer place to live and take the subway!

We can all agree that traffic jams are no fun. And breathing dirty air is no picnic either. Wouldn't you agree? Today, I'm going to tell you why you should take the subway to work in the morning. First, I'll talk about why it's more convenient. Then...

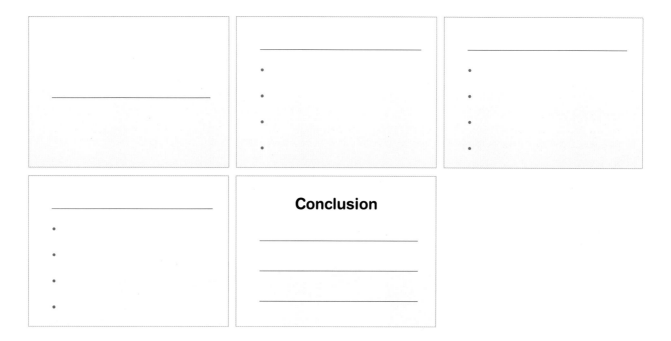

B   Give a short speech stating why one object or method is better than another. Use your notes from A.

Checklist

1   Besides using facts and data, how can someone strengthen an argument?
2   What is the benefit of choosing a topic you are knowledgeable about?
3   What method of collecting feedback from classmates is mentioned in the unit?
4   What four questions should you ask yourself when choosing a persuasive speech topic?

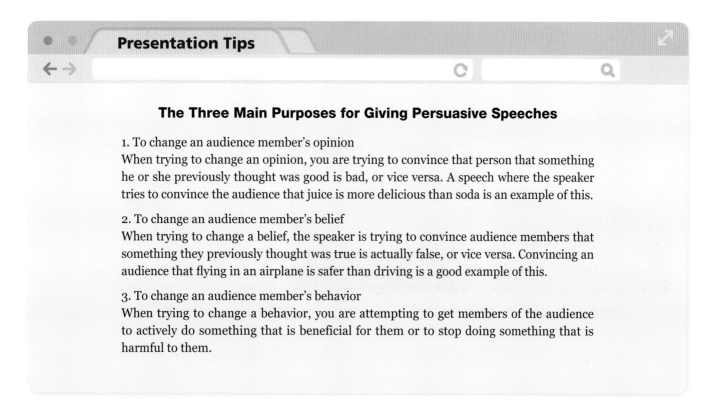

Presentation Tips

The Three Main Purposes for Giving Persuasive Speeches

1. To change an audience member's opinion
When trying to change an opinion, you are trying to convince that person that something he or she previously thought was good is bad, or vice versa. A speech where the speaker tries to convince the audience that juice is more delicious than soda is an example of this.

2. To change an audience member's belief
When trying to change a belief, the speaker is trying to convince audience members that something they previously thought was true is actually false, or vice versa. Convincing an audience that flying in an airplane is safer than driving is a good example of this.

3. To change an audience member's behavior
When trying to change a behavior, you are attempting to get members of the audience to actively do something that is beneficial for them or to stop doing something that is harmful to them.

Beliefs

Warm-up

Read the common myths and misconceptions. Then check the ones you used to believe in or still believe in now.

1

You should drink eight glasses of water per day. ☐

2

It takes seven years to digest swallowed chewing gum. ☐

3

Cracking your knuckles causes arthritis. ☐

4

Vitamin C prevents colds. ☐

5

Fortune cookies originated in China. ☐

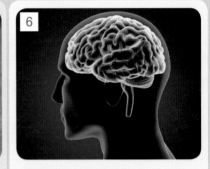

6

We only use 10% of our brains. ☐

7

The Great Wall of China is visible from outer space. ☐

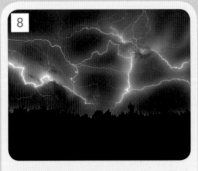

8

Lightning never strikes the same place twice. ☐

9

Bulls react to the color red. ☐

Myths and Misconceptions When writing a persuasive speech with the purpose of changing an audience member's beliefs, you can start by thinking about common myths and misconceptions in your culture. You can then present facts and data that prove these myths and misconceptions untrue.

Vocabulary

A   Match the words in the word box with the correct definitions.

data	evidence	fact	hypothesis	urban legend/myth

1 _____: a guess based on reasonable evidence about why something happens

2 _____: a scientific truth; something that can be proven

3 _____: proof that something is true or correct

4 _____: information that is measurable such as a statistic or a calculation

5 _____: a commonly held belief in a country or culture that is actually false

B   **Class activity | As a class, brainstorm some urban legends, myths, or misconceptions that are commonly held beliefs in your country.**

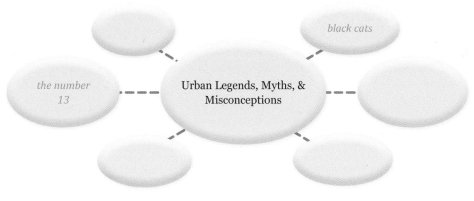

Grammar

A   Let's learn about using the verb *do*.

Negative	Questions	Tag Questions
I **don't** believe drinking eight glasses of water a day is necessary to be healthy.	How many glasses of water **do** you think we should drink in a day to be healthy?	You don't really think we need to drink eight glasses of water per day, **do** you?

Positive without *do*		Positive with *do* for Emphasis
I think we should drink eight glasses of water per day to be healthy.		I **do** think we should drink eight glasses of water per day to be healthy!

B   Complete the dialogue with the correct form of *do*.

A What ¹_____ you think about flying? ²_____ you think it's safer than driving?

B I ³_____ know. What ⁴_____ you think?

A Flying is definitely safer than driving.

B You ⁵_____ really believe that, ⁶_____ you?

A I ⁷_____ believe flying is safer than driving! Look at the data!

Stating Facts When providing supporting evidence during a speech, it is helpful to learn some words and expressions English speakers commonly use to state facts. When proving a commonly held belief untrue, it is important to present your evidence in a clear and understandable manner.

Language Patterns

A Let's learn some expressions for stating facts.

Stating Facts
It's true that…
The truth is that…
It has been proven that…
It's a fact that…
It is a well-known fact that…
It's a well-established fact that…
It's obvious that…
Actually…

B Use the expressions in A to complete the table with true facts by going online or by using facts that you already know to be true.

	Facts
1	*It's a well-known fact that whales are the largest mammals on the Earth.*
2	
3	
4	
5	

Pronunciation 🔊

A Read and listen to the sentences below. Then practice the common reductions for "It's a…" "He's a…" and "She's a…"

It's a…	*Itsa…*	**It's a** well-known fact that Jupiter is the largest planet.
He's a…	*Heeza…*	**He's a** famous researcher from MIT.
She's a…	*Sheeza…*	**She's a** chemist and inventor.

B Listen and practice the dialogues with a partner.

A Who is Neil deGrasse Tyson?

B **He's a** famous astrophysicist.

A Do you know who Katherine Freese is?

B Yes, I do. **She's a** famous astrophysicist, too. **She's an** expert on dark matter.

A What's dark matter?

B **It's a** very difficult thing to explain. I don't really understand it.

Supporting Facts When giving a persuasive speech with the purpose of changing an audience member's belief, using good supporting information is very important. In order to do this, you must do some research and find the most up-to-date and accurate data that supports your persuasive claim.

Reading 🔊

A Read about the interesting facts that might not be commonly understood.

Everyone knows that Mt. Everest is the highest mountain above sea level, but is it the tallest mountain on the Earth? No, it isn't. There is another mountain even taller than Everest in Hawaii called Mauna Kea. While Mt. Everest is 8,848 meters from base to peak, Mauna Kea is actually 10,200 meters from base to peak. The reason why Mt. Everest is better known than Mauna Kea is that more than half of Mauna Kea is underwater. With 5,995 meters of Mauna Kea submerged in the ocean, people don't realize just how stunningly tall it actually is.

Although many people believe driving or riding in a car is safer than flying, flying is actually the safest form of travel. Your odds of dying in a commercial air flight are 1 in 7 million. If you were to fly on an airplane every day of your life, you would need 19,000 years to experience a life-threatening accident. Traveling by car, however, is statistically much more dangerous. Every time you get into a car, you have a 1 in 14,000 chance of dying. It's obvious which method of travel is safer.

Following the Reading Fill in the blanks with the correct information.

Mt. Everest vs. Mauna Kea	Air Travel vs. Car Travel
• Mt. Everest is [1]_____ mountain above sea level. • Mt. Everest is 8,848 meters from [2]_____ to [3]_____. • Mauna Kea is [4]_____ meters from base to peak. • 5,995 meters of Mauna Kea are [5]_____ in the ocean.	• You would need 19,000 years to experience a life-[6]_____ accident in an airplane. • You have a 1 in 14,000 chance of [7]_____ in a [8]_____ accident. • You have a 1 in 7 million chance of dying in a [9]_____ flight accident.

B Which method of travel do you think is the best, and why?

I prefer traveling by airplane because it's fast and efficient. I'm not afraid of flying because I know that other methods of travel are more dangerous than flying.

Writing a Persuasive Claim When delivering a persuasive speech, you have to make a strong persuasive claim. The persuasive claim is your side of the controversial topic being discussed. It is your responsibility as the speaker to clearly state your side of the argument in the introduction.

A Match the persuasive claims to their general topics by writing the topics in the spaces provided.

Albert Einstein	Air Travel	Brain Capacity	The Five Senses
The Great Wall of China	Vision	Water	Flies

	General Topic	Persuasive Claim
1		It's a well-known fact that we use far more than 10% of it.
2		The truth is that it is not visible from space.
3		Actually, he was an excellent math student in school.
4		The truth is that it is much safer than driving a car.
5		It's a well-established fact that their lifespan is much longer than 24 hours.
6		It has been proven that we have a lot more than five of them.
7		Actually, eating carrots doesn't improve your eyesight.
8		It's obvious that we don't need to consume 8 glasses a day to be healthy.

It is a well-established fact that human beings use far more than 10% of their brain capacity.

B   Read the statements below, and write persuasive claims that disagree with them. Use the expressions for stating facts that we learned in the unit when writing your persuasive claims.

1   You should be extra careful on Friday the 13ᵗʰ because it is an unlucky day.

Actually, you are no more likely to have an accident on Friday the 13ᵗʰ than on any other day.

2   Shaving causes hair to grow back darker and thicker.

3   Cracking your knuckles causes arthritis.

4   Fortune cookies originated in China.

5   It takes seven years to digest a piece of swallowed chewing gum.

6   Black cats are bad luck.

7   Lightning never strikes the same place twice.

8   Taking vitamin C helps prevent colds.

C   Choose a controversial belief that many people in your country hold, and write it out as a statement. Read your statement to a small group and let your group members agree or disagree with it.

Your Statement

Ghosts exist, so we should be careful not to upset them.

Ghosts exist, so we should be careful not to upset them.

That's ridiculous! It's a well-established fact that ghosts are not real.

It's true that ghosts exist. I saw one when I was eleven years old.

🗨 **Common Mistakes lightning vs. lightening**

Lightning: an electric release which occurs during a thunderstorm

Lightening: making lighter or less dark; brightening

Do It Yourself

The Persuasive Speech: Beliefs Now it is time for you to do it yourself! Use the information you learned in the previous sections in order to create an outline for a speech that challenges a common belief.

A Write an attention-getting opener for the topic "Challenging a Common Belief." Think about which attention-getting opener strategy would best introduce your topic. After that, write your own persuasive claim and notes on some notecards.

Attention-Getting Opener + Persuasive Claim

Which common belief would you like to challenge in a short persuasive speech to your classmates?

Which strategy would you choose for your attention-getting opener?
☐ Tell a Story ☐ Use a Quotation from a Famous Person ☐ Ask a Rhetorical Question
☐ State a Shocking Fact or Statistic ☐ Use an Image ☐ Use a Gimmick, a Prop, or a Visual Aid

Now, write your attention-getting opener.

Persuasive Claim:

Attention-Getting Opener:
Has anyone ever told you that Einstein wasn't a good student?

Preview:
• origin of myth
• teenage years
• contributions to science

Origin of the Myth
• slow to start speaking as a child
• parents took him to a doctor
• began speaking at four

Teenage Years
• could solve complicated arithmetic problems by 12
• had mastered differential and integral calculus by 15

Contributions
• Theory of Relativity
• $E = mc^2$
• atomic energy

Summary
• why people believe this
• teen years
• Einstein's importance

Concluding Remarks:
As you can see, Einstein was brilliant, even as a student.

We can all agree that Einstein was a brilliant man. But has anyone ever told you that he wasn't a good student? Today, I'm going to tell you why it isn't true. First, I will talk about the origin of this myth. Next, I'll tell you about his teenage years. Finally, I'll talk about his wonderful scientific contributions.

Attention-Getting Opener:

Preview:
-
-
-

_____
-
-
-

_____
-
-
-

_____
-
-
-

Summary
-
-
-

Concluding Remarks:

B Give a short speech challenging a common belief. Use your notes from A.

Checklist

1 When writing a persuasive speech with the purpose of changing an audience member's belief, what can I start thinking about in order to find a good topic?

2 Give two examples of expressions English speakers use when stating facts.

3 When writing supporting details for a persuasive speech, what kind of data should you find?

4 What is a persuasive claim?

Presentation Tips

Pathos: Appealing to the Audience's Emotions

When building an argument, it is important to consider the idea of pathos. Pathos occurs when a speaker gets an emotional response from the audience. This tool of persuasive speaking requires the speaker to show a lot of emotion during a speech. By using emotions effectively, the speaker can get the audience to agree with his or her argument. The most effective way to use pathos is for the speaker to choose a topic he or she is very passionate about. Then there is a built-in emotional connection to the topic for the speaker. It is also important for pathos to be authentic. Trying to manipulate an audience by using emotions can cause the speaker to lose the trust of the audience. A speaker who is giving a speech about a topic that he or she is truly passionate about will get the best emotional reaction from the audience.

Behaviors

Warm-up

Circle the images below that you think show good habits and put an X through the ones that show bad habits.

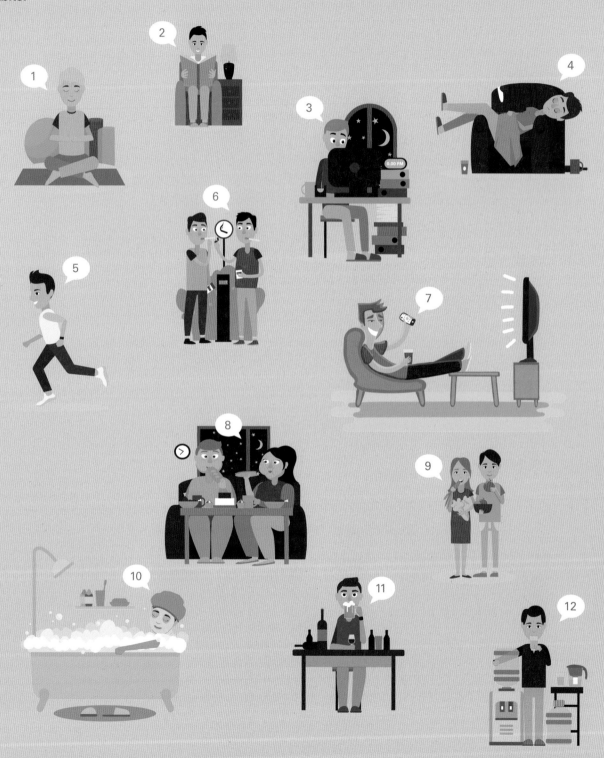

Problems and Solutions When giving a speech about changing a behavior, you might want to start by addressing a bad habit or a common problem people struggle with. Then you want to make a strong argument about why the person needs to overcome the challenge.

Vocabulary

A Match the harmful behaviors and disorders with the correct pictures.

| bad posture | heavy drinking | insomnia | overeating | phone addiction | smoking |

B **Speaking** | Do you have any of these problems? Which ones?

I'm addicted to my smartphone. I probably check my smartphone once a minute.

Grammar

A Let's learn about using bare infinitives when giving advice.

should / shouldn't + bare infinitive	Rhetorical Question Why don't you + bare infinitive
Everyone should **try** to donate blood. You shouldn't **arrive** late to a job interview.	Why don't you **try** working out at home? Why don't you **take** 30 minutes each day to study English?

B Complete the sentences with the correct bare infinitives from the word box.

| buy | call | start | quit |

1 You shouldn't _____ Brian anymore. He doesn't want to talk to you.

2 Should Junyoung and Melissa _____ dating? They'd make the perfect couple.

3 Do you think I should _____ these pants? They're expensive, but they look good.

4 Why don't you _____ smoking? It would really improve your quality of life.

Giving Advice When giving a speech about changing a behavior, you want to provide good advice to your audience. There are several common English expressions associated with giving advice.

Language Patterns

A Let's learn some expressions for giving advice.

Giving Advice	
You should go to sleep at a reasonable time. **I think you should** call her. (↔ I don't think you should call her.) **Why don't you** go to the doctor? **If I were you, I would** study harder for the next exam.	**How about** work**ing** as a freelancer? **I recommend/suggest** us**ing** public transportation. **It would be a good idea to** talk to your parents before you make a decision.

B **Pair work** | Ask your partner for advice by using the problems in the table. Give your partner advice by using the expressions in A.

	Problems
1	I really want to quit smoking. What should I do?
2	I want to get in shape, but I don't have much free time. What should I do?
3	I'm too stressed. What should I do to relax?
4	I can't sleep at night because I have insomnia. What should I do?
5	I want to date my best friend's ex. What should I do?

*ex = ex-boyfriend or ex-girlfriend

A I really want to quit smoking. What should I do?

B If I were you, I would buy some nicotine gum.

Pronunciation 🔊

A Read and listen to the sentences below. Then practice the common reductions often used for *shouldn't have* and *shouldn't*.

shouldn't	shouldn't have
shount /shoudynt He **shouldn't** yell at his dog.	*shounta /shoudynta /shoudyntuv* You **shouldn't have** been late.

B Listen and practice the dialogues.

1 A I can't believe you missed your final exam. You **shouldn't have** done that.
  B I know. But I'm going to ask my professor to give me another chance.

2 A You **shouldn't** smoke. It's not good for you.
  B I know, but it's really hard to quit.

3 A Your friend **shouldn't have** asked you for a loan.
  B I agree. You **shouldn't** lend money to a friend because it can affect the friendship negatively.

Supporting Details and Information As with any speech, it is important to provide strong supporting evidence in order to strengthen your argument. This can include experts' opinions, data, and other research you have done in preparation for your speech.

Reading 🔊

Read about one positive and one negative behavior.

Donating blood is one of the most important things we can do to help people. Only 10% of the population in the United States donates blood each year; however, any one of us could need blood at some point in our lives. Hospitals need people to donate blood for two very important reasons. First, blood can only be stored in hospitals for a short time. Doctors and surgeons cannot use blood that is too old. Second, a lot of medical procedures and surgeries require donated blood. Blood that is lost during surgery needs to be replaced. So why don't you save a life and donate blood?

- Michael Cho

I am worried that I might be experiencing some of the warning signs of smartphone addiction. The first sign is when you feel the need to constantly look at your phone. I probably check my phone at least once a minute, so I definitely experience the first sign. The second sign is when you think about your cell phone even when you are not using it. I do this, too. I think about who might be texting me, or whether or not I've just received a message on an SNS site. The last sign is when feelings of anger or depression occur because you can't use your phone. I don't feel angry or depressed when I can't use my phone, but I worry that I might have those feelings in the future.

- Heather Lim

Following the Reading Fill in the blanks with the correct information.

Blood Donation	Smartphone Addiction
• ¹_____ of Americans donate blood each year. • Blood can only be stored for a ²_____ time. • A lot of medical ³_____ and surgeries require donated blood.	3 Signs & Symptoms • You feel the need to constantly ⁴_____ at your phone. • You ⁵_____ about your phone when you are not using it. • You feel anger and ⁶_____ when you are unable to use your phone. Signs and Symptoms Heather Has Experienced • She looks at her phone ⁷_____ a minute. • She thinks about who might be ⁸_____ her. • She doesn't feel ⁹_____ or depressed yet.

Building on an Area of Agreement When writing a persuasive speech, it is important to create an opener which builds on an area of agreement. An area of agreement is a goal or objective that everyone in the audience agrees with; however, they might disagree with you on how to achieve that goal or objective.

A Read the different openers which build on areas of agreement. Then complete the openers by writing the letters of the correct persuasive claims in the boxes.

> a I think parents and teachers should complete four hours of online education regarding bullying and school violence.
> b I think becoming a vegetarian is the best choice a person can make.
> c I think men and women should both participate in mandatory military service.
> d I believe that soda and unhealthy snacks should no longer be sold on school grounds.

Famous actor Joaquin Phoenix said, "It takes nothing away from a human to be kind to an animal." No one wants animals to suffer unnecessarily...

Approximately 3 out of 4 students will experience some form of bullying. Now, everyone wants children to feel safe when they go to school. In order to achieve this goal...

Nearly 1 in 5 children aged 6 to 19 in the United States is obese. Everybody would like our children to be healthy, so...

All healthy adult males in South Korea must serve in the military. We all want to live in a fair and just society as well as have our country protected, so...

B Read the persuasive claims. Then write a sentence that builds on an area of agreement. You can start your sentences with: *We all want, Everyone, Everybody, No one, Nobody*.

ex.	Area of Agreement	*We all want our children to be safe when they are at school.*
	Persuasive Claim	Principals and teachers should be able to look inside students' bags or backpacks anytime during the school day without the students' permission.
1	Area of Agreement	
	Persuasive Claim	Parents shouldn't punish their children by spanking them.
2	Area of Agreement	
	Persuasive Claim	You should never lend large amounts of money to a friend.
3	Area of Agreement	
	Persuasive Claim	The legal drinking age should be raised to 22.
4	Area of Agreement	
	Persuasive Claim	Zoos should be banned.
5	Area of Agreement	
	Persuasive Claim	The government should provide free housing to homeless people.

We all want our children to be safe when they are at school. So that's why I think principals and teachers should be able to look inside students' bags or backpacks without the students' permission.

Common Mistakes principal & principle

principal = the president or leader of a school

principle = a fundamental belief or ideal

Do It Yourself

The Persuasive Speech: Behaviors Now it is time for you to do it yourself! Use the information you learned in the previous sections in order to create an outline for a speech that encourages the audience to change a behavior.

A Write an attention-getting opener for the topic "Changing a Behavior." Think about which attention-getting opener strategy would best introduce your topic. Use the form below to outline your speech.

Attention-Getting Opener + Building on an Area of Agreement

What behavior would you like to encourage the audience to change?

Which strategy would you choose for your attention-getting opener?

☐ Tell a Story ☐ Use a Quotation from a Famous Person ☐ Ask a Rhetorical Question

☐ State a Shocking Fact or Statistic ☐ Use an Image ☐ Use a Gimmick, a Prop, or a Visual Aid

Now, write your attention-getting opener.

Look at the example of an opener which builds on an area of agreement. Then look at the persuasive claim. Complete the outline below with information about your speech topic.

ex. We all want to feel healthy, don't we? | In order to feel our best, we should stop smoking cigarettes.

Area of Agreement | Persuasive Claim

Write your opener which builds on an area of agreement.

*We all want... / Everyone can agree that... / No one wants...

Area of Agreement:

Write your persuasive claim here.

Persuasive Claim:

Preview of Main Points:

Main Point 1:

Main Point 2:

Main Point 3:

Summary:

Concluding Remarks:

B Give a short speech encouraging the audience members to change a behavior. Use your notes from A.

Checklist

1 How might you start a speech whose purpose is to change a behavior?

2 Give three examples of expressions used to give advice.

3 Where can a speaker find strong supporting evidence?

4 In a persuasive speech, what must the opener do other than grab the audience's attention?

5 How can we define an area of agreement?

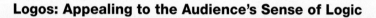

Presentation Tips

Logos: Appealing to the Audience's Sense of Logic

Logos is an important part of persuasive speaking. Logos occurs when you have built a strong logical foundation for your argument. It is easy for speakers to get caught up in the emotional aspect of a speech. But an emotional appeal will not work unless the basis for your argument is sound. Logos can be achieved when you have done the following:

• researched your topic well
• included good supporting evidence in your speech
• explained the evidence to the audience in a clear and well-organized manner

Each piece of evidence should help you build a stronger case. The evidence should also be relevant to the topic and support the persuasive claim. When all of the pieces have come together, a strong logical argument will have been made.

Warm-up

Match the words in the word box to the correct pictures.

| area chart | bar chart | column chart | line chart | pie chart | Venn diagram |

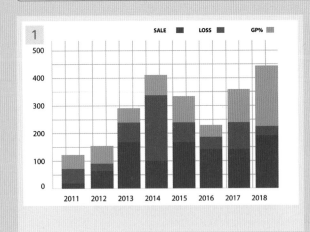

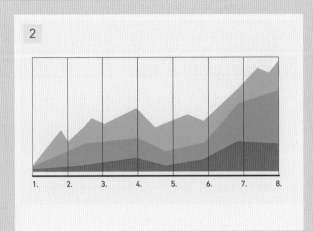

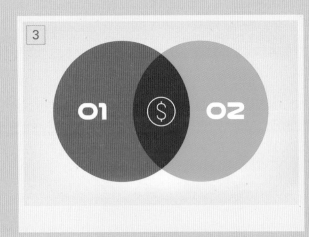

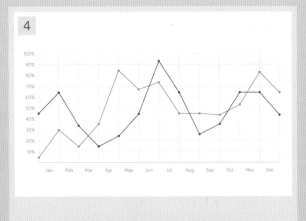

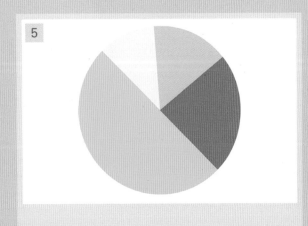

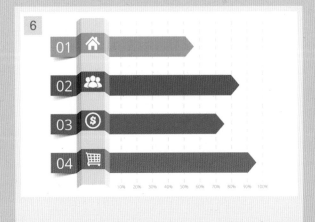

Conducting Research When writing the speech, you may need to conduct research in order to find appropriate supporting evidence for your speech. Once you have done your research, you can display the data you have collected visually through the use of charts or graphs.

Vocabulary

A   Match the words with the correct pictures.

| dictionary | encyclopedia | library | mass media | online research | survey |

B   **Class activity** | Write down your top five favorite types of cuisine (Thai, Indian, Italian, Korean, Mexican, Chinese, Japanese, etc.). Then ask each student in the class which type of cuisine from your list is his or her favorite. Once you have collected your data, make a column chart, bar chart, or pie chart showing your data.

Grammar

A   Let's learn about reported speech.

Direct Quote	Reported Speech
Alicia: "The graph **shows** an uptick in sales in 2018."	Alicia said the graph **showed** an uptick in sales in 2018.
My professor: "The stock market **crashed** in 1929."	My professor said that the stock market **had crashed** in 1929.
Juyoon: "I **will** look for information online."	Juyoon said he **would** look for information online.

B   Read the direct quotes out loud as reported speech.

1   Daphne: "The pie chart shows the percentage of university students with student debt."

2   Akira: "Workers' wages dropped in 2017."

3   Professor Moon: "The country will see a rise in unemployment in 2019."

Citing Sources When giving a speech, it is important to cite the sources you used in the speech. Speakers do this to give credit to the experts and authors whose work they are using in their speeches. It also tells the audience that they are honest and trustworthy.

Language Patterns

A Let's learn about citing source material in a speech.

Direct Quotations	Jane Goodall **said**, "What you do makes a difference."
Books (title & author)	**According to** Jaeyon Shin, the **author of** *The Future of Energy*, 50% of the country's energy will be clean by 2080.
Websites	The website www.solarlife.org **states that** China made more solar panels than any other country in 2017.

B **Pair work** | **Choose box 1 or 2. Then practice citing the sources to a partner by using the expressions in A.**

1	2
Ferdinand Porsche: "I couldn't find the sports car of my dream, so I built it myself."	Gene Tunney: "To enjoy the glow of good health, you must exercise."
Author: Gary Miller	Author: Rachel de Leon
Title: *The History of Cars*	Title: *The Obesity Epidemic*
Text: The Ford Motor Company installed the first assembly line in 1913.	Text: Almost 20% of children in the United States are obese.
Website: www.carstatistics.com	Website: www.healthyliving.gov
Text: 18 million new cars and trucks were sold in 2016.	Text: 9 out of 10 teenagers do not get enough exercise.

Pronunciation 🔊

A Read and listen to the common pronunciations of these numbers. Then practice the sentences by reading them aloud.

13, 14, 15, 16, 17, 18, 19 soft /n/ ending sound	30, 40, 50, 60, 70, 80, 90 /i/ ending sound
14 out of 20 students like Indian food. Dr. Barton's book came out in **2016**. Stores shouldn't sell violent video games to anyone under the age of **19**.	According to the book *Mars: The Future of Travel*, Dr. Marianna de Cruz states that we will travel to Mars by **2060**. According to some experts, **40**% of cars will be electric by **2050**.

B Listen and circle the correct numbers.

1 a. 2013   b. 2030
2 a. 150   b. 115
3 a. 90   b. 19

4 a. 3,416   b. 3,460
5 a. 18   b. 80

Discussing Visual Aids When using visual aids, it is best to discuss the visual aids conversationally (extemporaneously) with the audience. This shows the audience that you know what you are talking about and that you are the expert with regard to the topic being discussed.

Reading 🔊

A Read the paragraphs that describe the visual aids.

We all want to look good and feel healthy. But in order to maintain a physically fit body, exercise isn't the only thing we need to consider. According to Kelly Martinez, the author of the book *Eating Right: How to Eat Healthfully in the 21ˢᵗ Century*, what we eat is actually more important than how much exercise we do. In order to have a healthy body, we need to focus 70% of our energy on diet and 30% of our energy on exercise. This was very helpful for me. You see, I had been exercising a lot, but I wasn't losing any weight. The problem was that my diet wasn't very good. When I started eating right, I began to lose weight.

- Bella / 31

We all know that apartment prices in the country are too high. The website www.housingdepartment.gov states that there was a steady increase in apartment prices last year, and it looks like apartment prices will continue to rise this year, too. Since workers' wages and salaries have not increased in the past five years, young couples cannot afford to buy homes. These days, most young couples rent apartments instead of buying them.

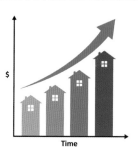

Following the Reading Change the incorrect sentences into correct ones.

1 We should focus 30% of our energy on nutrition.

2 Bella had been exercising a lot, so she lost weight.

3 Apartment prices have stabilized.

4 Workers' wages and salaries have increased in the past five years.

5 These days, most young couples buy homes instead of renting them.

B How much energy do you focus on diet and nutrition? How about exercise? Complete the pie chart below with a visual representation of your lifestyle.

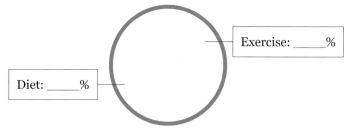

Describing Changes in Charts and Graphs When using visual aids, you must be able to describe changes or trends in the charts and graphs. There are phrases and expressions that you can use to describe specific changes.

A **Match the statements to the correct charts and graphs.**

> a The website www.coffeeconsumer.com states that **25%** of the coffee sold in the country comes from South America.
>
> b According to Bill Bryson, the author of *The Solar Energy Success Story*, the production of solar panels in China has **increased dramatically**.
>
> c Janine Tyson said, "**20%** of Americans would like to have faster Internet connections."
>
> d According to Hyemin Jung, the author of the book *Korea and the Semiconductor Business*, the price of semiconductors has **fluctuated slightly** over the past ten years.
>
> e CEO Tom Redford said, "Global oil prices have **fluctuated wildly** over the past five years."
>
> f The website www.bikes.com states that sales of bikes in the USA have **decreased dramatically**.

1
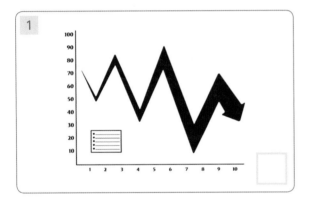

2

3

4
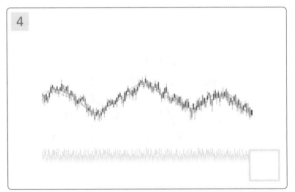

5

6

B Complete the comments based on the information in the charts and graphs.

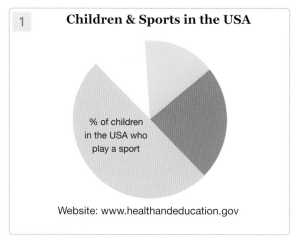

1 Children & Sports in the USA

% of children
in the USA who
play a sport

Website: www.healthandeducation.gov

The website www.healthandeducation.gov states
that [a]_____% of children in the [b]_____
play a [c]_____.

2 Car Production in Japan

1980   1990

Author: James Gleeson
Book: *The History of Car Production in Japan*

According to [a]_____, the author of
[b]_____, car production
in Japan [c]_____ dramatically from 1980
to 1990.

3 Coal Use in China

Quote: "Coal use in China has decreased
dramatically." - Chen Luan

[a]_____ said, "[b]_____ use
in China has [c]_____ dramatically."

4 Cost of Electricity in the U.K.

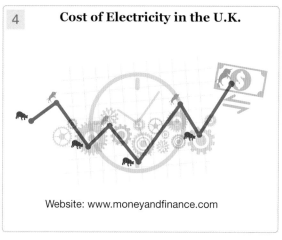

Website: www.moneyandfinance.com

The [a]_____ www.moneyandfinance.com
states that the [b]_____ of electricity in the
United Kingdom has [c]_____ wildly.

⚠ **Common Mistakes** said (past tense "not habitual") vs. says (present tense and "habitual")

Our professor said, "Coal use in China has decreased in recent years."

Our professor says, "Don't ask me for the answer. Look it up!"

Do It Yourself

The Informative or Persuasive Speech: Using Visual Aids and Putting It All Together

Now it is time for you to do it yourself. Use the information you learned in the previous sections in order to create an outline for a speech that requires the use of a visual aid.

A Choose a topic, informative or persuasive, in which you need to conduct a small amount of research in order to write the speech.

1. What is your speech topic and purpose?

☐ to inform the audience   ☐ to persuade the audience (change an opinion/a belief/a behavior)

If you decide to inform the audience, refer to 1-1. And if you decide to persuade the audience, refer to 1-1 and 1-2.

1-1. Which strategy would you choose for your attention-getting opener?

☐ Tell a Story   ☐ Use a Quotation from a Famous Person   ☐ Ask a Rhetorical Question

☐ State a Shocking Fact or Statistic   ☐ Use an image   ☐ Use a Gimmick, a Prop, or a Visual Aid

1-2. What is your opener which builds on an area of agreement? And what is your persuasive claim?

Area of Agreement:

Persuasive Claim:

2. What three main points are you going to preview?

"Today, I will talk about _____, _____, and _____."

3. Which brainstorming strategy would you choose for the body portion of your speech?

☐ mind-mapping   ☐ jotting down notes   ☐ free-writing

4. Which do you plan to use?

☐ PowerPoint slides   ☐ notecards   ☐ both

5. If you use visual aids,

5-1. What kind of research do you need to conduct in order to create your visual aid?

☐ a survey   ☐ online research   ☐ library research   ☐ mass media

☐ encyclopedia/dictionary

5-2. What kind of visual aids would you like to include in your speech?

☐ an area chart   ☐ a bar chart   ☐ a column chart   ☐ a line chart

☐ a pie chart   ☐ a diagram

Main Point 1:

Main Point 2:

Main Point 3:

Summary:

Concluding Remarks:

B Give a short informative or persuasive speech.

> **Introduction**
> Attention-Getting Opener + Preview of Main Points
> If the speech is persuasive,
> 1. Make sure your opener builds on an area of agreement.
> 2. Clearly state your persuasive claim.

> **Body**
> Main Points 1, 2, and 3
> (Include visuals such as charts or diagrams.)

> **Conclusion**
> Summary of Main Points + Concluding Remarks

Checklist

1 How can we display our data visually in a speech?

2 Why is it important to cite sources in a speech?

3 What three kinds of sources are mentioned in the unit?

4 Why is it important to discuss visual aids conversationally?

5 What must you be able to do when using visual aids?

Presentation Tips

Ethos: Appealing to the Audience's Sense of Ethics

Ethos is when we appeal to the audience's sense of ethics. The purpose of ethos is to establish credibility in the speaker and in the sources used in the speech. Unlike pathos and logos, ethos has to do with where we get our information from and whether the sources we use in the speech are credible. It asks the audience to accept us as credible speakers. In order to be credible, one must conduct the appropriate amount of research necessary to explain the topic honestly. This means that the speaker has found correct and up-to-date information. It also means that the experts cited during the speech are qualified experts in their fields of study. Charts and graphs should be accurate if we want to pass the ethical test. When we combine pathos, logos, and ethos together effectively, we can create a powerfully persuasive speech.

People

Building Content ❶ p.9

Vocabulary

A

1 d	2 b	3 f
4 g	5 a	6 c
7 e		

Grammar

B

1 What	2 Where	3 Why
4 When	5 Who	

Learning How p.12

A

1
  a 21
  b Atlanta
  c university student
  d design
  e interior decorating
  f a multinational interior design company
  g beautiful
  h thin
  i blond
  j fashionable

2
  a serious
  b funny
  c great sense of humor
  d friendly
  e cleaning his room on the weekend
  f playing online games with his brother
  g watching TV
  h listening to music
  i drinking alcohol

B

1

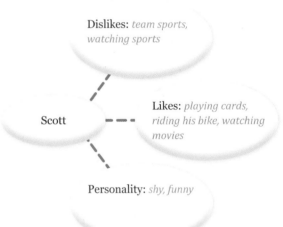

Hair: *short blond hair*

Eye Color: *light brown, hazel*

Amanda

Style: *cool, stylish, good fashion sense*

Other Features: *fair skin, pretty, a good figure*

2

Dislikes: *team sports, watching sports*

Likes: *playing cards, riding his bike, watching movies*

Scott

Personality: *shy, funny*

Checklist p.15

1 *What, who, where, when,* and *why* were mentioned.
2 You can discuss jobs, appearance, personality, likes and dislikes, hometown, and age.
3 You get to know the person on a deeper level.
4 No, you do not.
5 The mind map will help you create the body of the speech.
6 The introduction, body, and conclusion are the three main parts of a speech.

Precious Objects

Unit 2

Warm-up

p.16

1 ring, wedding
2 guitar, gift
3 necklace, grandmother
4 army, hat

Building Content ①

p.17

Vocabulary

A
1 inexpensive
2 broken
3 valuable
4 gigantic
5 antique
6 miniature

Grammar

B

1	2		2	2		3	1
4	2		5	2			

Building Content ③

p.19

Reading

Following the Reading

1 Her great-grandmother was the first to receive the family heirloom.
2 When she turns 13, she will probably receive the family heirloom.
3 She thinks it looks scary.
4 He will give his son the guitar.

Learning How

p.20

A
1 great-grandfather's
2 London
3 WWII
4 100
5 16
6 small
7 heavy
8 expensive
9 antique
10 scratched
11 30 years

B
1 locket with picture, mom wore it when I was young
2 shiny, heart-shaped, pretty, expensive

Checklist

p.23

1 We should use descriptive adjectives.
2 We should avoid using the same adjective again and again.
3 Feel, smell, sound, look, and taste are mentioned.
4 Jotting down notes is discussed.
5 Yes, it is.

Houses or Apartments

Unit 3

Warm-up

p.24

A
1 living room
2 bathroom
3 bedroom
4 dining room
5 kitchen
6 garage

Building Content ①

p.25

Vocabulary

A

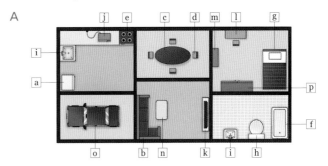

Grammar

B
1 There are
2 There is
3 Is there
4 There are
5 There is
6 Are there

Building Content ③

p.27

Reading

Following the Reading

Barbara's House: small, 2 bedrooms, 1 living room, 1 bathroom, suburbs, garden

Simon's Apartment: roomy, 3 bedrooms, 2 bathrooms, high ceilings, downtown

p.28

A

The Rooms and Their Spatial Relationships

There are five rooms in my house. There are a living room, a kitchen, a bedroom, a bathroom, and a dining room. The kitchen is next to the dining room. ~~My kitchen is really dirty right now. I need to do the dishes.~~ The dining room is next to the bedroom. The bedroom is across from the bathroom. The living room is across from the dining room. ~~I wish my dining room were bigger.~~

The Items and Their Spatial Relationships

There are a bed, a closet, a desk, and a bookcase in the bedroom. The desk is next to the bookcase. ~~I should reorganize my bookcase.~~ The bookcase is across from the bed. The closet is next to the bed. There are a sofa, a coffee table, and a TV in the living room. The TV is across from the sofa. The coffee table is between the sofa and the TV. ~~I think the television remote control is under the sofa.~~ There are a fridge, a microwave, and a stove in the kitchen. ~~I don't like cooking.~~ There are a dining table and four chairs in the dining room.

Interesting Facts about My House

I bought this house two years ago. It's the first house I've ever owned. There is a cute garden in the backyard. ~~My mother had a garden when I was young.~~ I grow squash, kale, and strawberries in my garden. My house is near a school. ~~The school has a soccer field and a basketball court.~~ My house is only five years old, so it's pretty new. My house is painted red, but I'm thinking about painting it blue this summer. ~~Blue is my favorite color.~~

B

(Example Answer)

There are a bedroom, a living room, a kitchen, a closet, and a bathroom in the apartment. The bedroom is next to the living room, and the kitchen is next to the bathroom. The bathroom is in front of the bedroom, and the living room is behind the kitchen and the closet. The closet is between the bathroom and the kitchen. There are a bed and two tables in the bedroom. The bed is between the tables. There are a tub, a sink, and a toilet in the bathroom. The sink is between the tub and the toilet. There are clothes in the closet. There are a stove, a fridge, a sink, a table, and two chairs in the kitchen. The fridge and the stove are across from the sink. The table is between the two chairs. There are a sofa, chairs, a coffee table, a plant, and a bookcase in the living room. The bookcase is next to the plant. The coffee table is in front of the sofa. The chairs are near the coffee table.

C

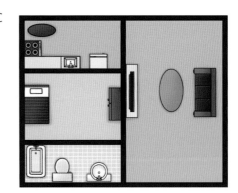

Checklist   p.31

1 It gives the listener a better mental image of the place.
2 Prepositions express spatial relationships between objects.
3 Location, design features, and personal significance are mentioned.
4 Don't edit your notes. Edit them at the end of the free-writing session.

Holidays

Unit **4**

p.33

Vocabulary

A

1 American Thanksgiving
2 Ramadan
3 Buddha's Birthday (The date may vary outside of Korea and China.)
4 Christmas
5 Thai Songkran Festival
6 Dia de los Muertos (Day of the Dead)

p.35

Reading

Following the Reading

1 He hangs Christmas lights.
2 She thinks it looks beautiful.
3 Her father plays the piano while her mother sings.
4 He usually spends Thanksgiving with his friends Cindy and Daniel.

5 They are college friends.

6 He likes seeing his closest friends.

p.36

Learning How

A

1 b, f   2 a, d   3 c, e

Checklist   p.39

1 They come before main verbs and after the "be" verb.

2 Adjectives ending in -ed reveal feelings, and ones ending in -ing reveal something that makes you feel a certain way.

3 You must grab the audience's attention.

4 Telling a story, quoting a famous person, and asking a rhetorical question are mentioned.

Food and Drinks

Unit 5

Warm-up   p.40

1 chef / d, f   2 baker / a, g

3 bartender / b, h   4 barista / c, e

Building Content ❶   p.41

Vocabulary

A

1 Put, in / 3   2 Read / 1

3 Chop up / 2   4 Serve / 5

5 Eat / 6   6 Add / 4

Building Content ❸   p.43

Reading

Following the Reading

1 She started when she was a freshman in college.

2 She recently purchased an espresso machine.

3 She has been baking for about five years.

4 She learned to bake at her local community center.

5 He enjoys craft beer/dark lager.

6 He likes talking with friends, sipping a cold beer, and relaxing.

Checklist   p.47

1 You should make sure you are using the correct verbs to describe the processes.

2 We use sequence words, so the listener knows in which order things should happen.

3 It personalizes the speech and makes it more interesting.

4 You could state a surprising fact or statistic, show a photo, or use a gimmick, prop, or other visual aid.

Sports and Exercise

Unit 6

Building Content ❶   p.49

Vocabulary

A

Grammar

B

1 must/have to   2 mustn't

3 must/have to   4 don't have to

5 mustn't   6 don't have to

Building Content ❸   p.51

Reading

Following the Reading

1 He does aerobics three times a week.

2 He pays money, so he feels like he has to go.

3 The studio is large, and he likes the floor.

4 She likes going to the beach and playing badminton.

5 She doesn't have to wear shoes.

6 People look at them strangely.

A

1 Use Bullet Points & Limit the Amount of Text / a
2 Use Good-Quality Graphics and Images / a
3 Clearly Contrast Your Text and Background Colors / b

Checklist   p.55

1 You should include a list of the items you need to do the sport.
2 "Must not" means you are not allowed to do something, but "don't have to" means you have the choice to do something.
3 We say play basketball, do Pilates, and go skiing.
4 It can enhance the quality of the speech or presentation.
5 Clearly contrast your text and background colors, use bullet points and limit the amount of text, and use good-quality graphics and images.

Natural Processes   Unit 7

Warm-up   p.56

1 seeds	2 sprout
3 tree	4 flower
5 fruit	6 egg
7 caterpillar	8 pupa
9 butterfly	10 infant
11 child	12 adolescent
13 adult	

Building Content ❶   p.57

Vocabulary

A

1 seed	2 life cycle
3 pupa/chrysalis	4 reproduce
5 offspring	6 siblings

Grammar

B

1 Have, seen	2 haven't been
3 have taken	4 Have, raised

Building Content ❸   p.59

Reading

Following the Reading

1 False	2 True
3 False	4 False
5 True	6 True

Learning How   p.60

A

1 b	2 b	3 a

B

1 a eggs		b hatchling
c juvenile		d adult
2 a infancy		b childhood
c adolescence		d adulthood
3 a starts		b a seed
c turns into		d a plant
e vines		f flowers
g develop into		h become
i pumpkins		

Checklist   p.63

1 We call it a life cycle.
2 We can use *begin with, start with, develop into, grow into,* and *become.*
3 It gives the audience a better understanding of the topic.
4 Don't use more than six bullet points in a single slide, don't read the slide, and don't change the background colors of the slides.
5 It can diminish the quality of a speech.

Manmade Processes or Inventions   Unit 8

Warm-up   p.64

A

1 c	2 a	3 d
4 b		

Building Content ❶

p.65

Vocabulary

A

1 discovered
2 important
3 designed
4 Gadget
5 experiments
6 imagine

Grammar

B

1 Teflon
2 fidget spinner
3 Ford Model T
4 disposable diapers
5 paper

Building Content ❸

p.67

Reading

Following the Reading

1 generator → metal rod
2 not → ~~not~~
3 North America and Australia → South America and Africa
4 soft → hard

Learning How

p.68

A

1 d
2 e
3 a
4 b
5 c

B

1 inventor
2 benefits
3 Thomas Edison
4 1800s
5 Menlo Park
6 New Jersey
7 filament
8 glass bulb
9 glow
10 directions
11 dark in the evenings
12 productive
13 all night
14 how it works
15 website

Checklist

p.71

1 You should mention the inventor.
2 It is helpful to know if the effect of the process is helpful or harmful to society.
3 You should start at the beginning of the process and end with the last stage in the process.
4 They can help you remember key points.
5 Do underline important words and phrases, don't write messily or in small print, do number your cards, don't write out your speech word for word, and do use bullet points.

Opinions

Unit 9

Building Content ❶

p.73

Vocabulary

A

1 convenient
2 satisfying
3 enjoyable
4 useful
5 difficult, satisfied

Building Content ❷

p.74

Pronunciation

B

1 c
2 a
3 b
4 a
5 c

Building Content ❸

p.75

Reading

Following the Reading

1 He can appreciate the landscapes and geography more because buses move more slowly than airplanes do.
2 She thinks tablets are good learning tools.
3 Her son likes to color pictures on her tablet.
4 She likes it because it saves her time.
5 She hopes someone will invent a robotic mop.

Learning How

p.76

A

1 d
2 a
3 b
4 c

Checklist

p.79

1 You can strengthen an argument by including your personal experience with a topic.
2 It shortens the research time.
3 The speaker can conduct a survey in order to collect feedback.
4 You should ask yourself if it is personal to you, if you know who your audience is, if what you are asking your audience to do is possible, and whether or not your topic

is interesting or controversial.

Beliefs

Building Content 1

p.81

Vocabulary

A
1 hypothesis   2 fact
3 evidence   4 data
5 urban legend/myth

Grammar

B
1 do   2 Do   3 don't
4 do   5 don't   6 do
7 do

Building Content 3

p.83

Reading

Following the Reading
1 the highest   2 base
3 peak   4 10,200
5 submerged   6 threatening
7 dying   8 car
9 commercial

Learning How

p.84

A
1 Brain Capacity
2 The Great Wall of China
3 Albert Einstein
4 Air Travel
5 Flies
6 The Five Senses
7 Vision
8 Water

Checklist

p.87

1 Start thinking about some common cultural myths and misconceptions.
2 "It's a fact that…" and "The truth is that…" are examples of language used to state facts.
3 The most up-to-date and accurate data
4 A persuasive claim is the persuasive speaker's side of a particular issue.

Behaviors

Building Content 1

p.89

Vocabulary

A
1 phone addiction   2 bad posture
3 smoking   4 overeating
5 heavy drinking   6 insomnia

Grammar

B
1 call   2 start   3 buy
4 quit

Building Content 3

p.91

Reading

Following the Reading
1 10%   2 short
3 procedures   4 look
5 think   6 depression
7 once   8 texting
9 angry

Learning How

p.92

A
1 b   2 a   3 d
4 c

B
(Example Answer)
1 Everyone wants their children to be well-behaved and respectful.
2 Everybody wants to have good relationships with their friends.

3 No one wants young people to be addicted to alcohol.

4 No one wants to make animals suffer.

5 Everybody deserves to have a home.

Checklist
p.95

1 You can start by addressing bad habits or common problems.

2 When giving advice, you could use expressions such as "Why don't you..." "If I were you, I would..." and "How about..."

3 You can include experts' opinions, data, and other research.

4 It must also build on areas of agreement.

5 An area of agreement is a goal or an objective that everyone in the audience would agree with.

Research and Visual Aids
Unit 12

Warm-up
p.96

1 column chart

2 area chart

3 Venn diagram

4 line chart

5 pie chart

6 bar chart

Building Content 1
p.97

Vocabulary

A

1 encyclopedia

2 survey

3 mass media

4 dictionary

5 online research

6 library

Grammar

B

1 Daphne said the pie chart showed the percentage of university students with student debt.

2 Akira said workers' wages had dropped in 2017.

3 Professor Moon said that the country would see a rise in unemployment in 2019.

Building Content 2
p.98

Pronunciation

B

1 a   2 b   3 a

4 b   5 b

Building Content 3
p.99

Reading

Following the Reading

1 nutrition → exercise

2 so she lost → but she didn't lose

3 stabilized → increased

4 have increased → have not increased

5 buy → rent / renting → buying

Learning How
p.100

A

1 e   2 b   3 a

4 d   5 f   6 c

B

1 a 50
  b USA
  c sport

2 a James Gleeson
  b The History of Car Production in Japan
  c increased

3 a Chen Luan
  b Coal
  c decreased

4 a website
  b cost
  c fluctuated

Checklist
p.103

1 We can use a chart or graph.

2 By citing sources, we give credit to the experts and authors whose work we are using in our speeches. It also makes us look trustworthy to the audience.

3 Quotes, books, and websites are mentioned.

4 It shows the audience that you know what you're talking about.

5 You must be able to describe trends or changes.